THE RED DRAGON'S TAIL – PROPHETS WHO TEACH LIES

By Donald A. Peart

ISBN: 9798744051853

REFERENCES

All scriptures happen to be quoted from the New International Version, unless otherwise noted.

All parenthetical notes, underscoring, and bold lettering of the Scriptures in this text are supplied by this author. They are supplied for emphasis and clarity. Some words in the King James Version (now in "Public Domain") are updated to read as modern English.

Dictionary References

Strong's Exhaustive Concordance
Vines Expository Dictionary
BibleSoft Software

ACKNOLEDGMENT

The Lord Jesus is preeminent in everything. All that is accomplished through His Church is a direct result of His grace. He is the resurrected Lord. He is the real, living flesh and bone Jesus at the right hand of the Heavenly Father interceding for us. We are not serving dumb idols. Because the heavenly Father is the living God, He communicates with us. Therefore, I give tribute to the Spirit of the living Son, Jesus, the Christ, who is still speaking in us.

Special thanks to my beautiful wife Judith and the six children the Lord gave us (Donald Jr. and Keyanna (his wife), Jeshua, Charity, Benjamin, and Jesse). Judith, I appreciate the liberty you have afforded me to write because of your understanding of the will of the Lord.

Thanks to the Church family we shepherd for supplying their measure. We are laborers together in the work of our Lord Jesus Christ. It is my prayer that great grace continues to be upon them and that you may stand mature and fully-wear all the will of God.

TABLE OF CONTENTS

PREFACE

I greet you in the name of our Lord Jesus Christ. The Spirit of the Lord has directed me to write concerning the prophets who teach lies and the false prophet—a beast spirit—who energizes them. His first directive came in the mid 1990s. He said, "Send it to the seven Churches sown across the land."

The Lord instructed me to "prophesy against the false prophet and <u>cast</u> him down." I am to "speak to his (the false prophet's) purposes and prophesy his demise." This command was executed in the first book, *The False Prophet, Alias, Another Beast.*

I have, therefore, set forth in order this other synoptic book in keeping with the Lord Jesus instruction. The book is brief for many reasons. One of the reasons is that most of the youth of today do not have the patience to read extensive writings.

This book is catering to their need that they might have an understanding about the many false prophets, so as not to be deceived. However, for the person who enjoys serious study, there are many references. These references will assist the serious student and broaden his or her understanding.

It is also my desire that all readers read the entire series—*The False Prophet, Alias, Another Beast, Son of Man Prophesy Against the False Prophet and Cast Him Down*, and this volume—for a more complete understanding of the spirit of the false prophet and the beast associated with the false prophet.

This is because some of the teachings of the series were hidden from other generations; however, the Holy Spirit is now revealing these mysteries to His Church through His holy apostles and prophets.

I pray that this book may be enlightening to you, strengthening your resistance against the many false prophets, by the anointing in you. Finally, I also pray that the fifth chapter encourages you to receive the true apostolic and prophetic ministries.

Donald A. Peart
Called of God, "a son!"

TWO HORNS LIKE A LAMB

Revelation 13:11, NIV: Then I saw another beast, coming out of the earth. **He had two horns like a lamb**, *but* **he spoke like a dragon**.

1 John 4:1, NIV: Dear friends, **do not believe every spirit,** *but test the spirits to see whether they are from God, because* **many false prophets** *have gone out into the world.*

Matthew 7:15, NIV: Watch out for **false prophets.** *They come to you in* **sheep's clothing,** *but inwardly they are ferocious wolves.*

One of the challenges of this age for Jesus' disciples will be to discern the many false prophets who are among us and, and with that discerning ability, still function in the Spirit and in the love of God amid the apparent contradictions. (Genesis 41; Daniel 2; Exodus 7; John 6:70-71). As I cite some examples of how to discern the false ones, I will first demonstrate how they dress.

False prophets like to wear "sheep's clothing." The Scriptures above gave some explicit description concerning an entity called "another beast" (Revelation 13:11), alias, "the false prophet" (Revelation 16:13; Revelation 20:10). This being is called a "beast;" however, this same beast has "two horns like a lamb."

Revelation 13:11, NIV: Then I saw another beast, coming out of the earth. **He had two horns like a lamb**, *but* **he spoke like a dragon**.

He also speaks "like a dragon." These descriptions, beloved, are symbols of the false prophet's character. In every generation, there are entities that have horns like "a lamb." That is, the false prophet has horns "like" Jesus, the Lamb of God, and His Church. Except, the Lamb of God, Jesus, has seven horns (complete power, the false prophet only has two (limited false witness power). In addition, the false prophet also speaks like "a dragon." Satan is called that "original serpent, the dragon" in

Revelation 12:9. Hence, the "another beast" who speaks like a dragon, speaks like Satan. He does not sound like a sheep! According to the verse previously cited, having "horns like a lamb" does not necessarily make the false prophet speaks like sheep (he speaks like a dragon), especially during adverse experiences. Compare Isaiah 53:7; I Peter 2:21-23 where we see how the Lamb of God functions as a sheep in adversity. It is the words from within that are spoken which determine the nature of that prophet, not the outward appearance. Allow me to explain.

SHEEP'S CLOTHING

Matthew 7:15, NIV: Watch out for false prophets. They come to you in **sheep's clothing,** *but inwardly they are ferocious wolves.*

Jesus said false prophets would come in "sheep's clothing." He did not say they would come "as sheep." False prophets are not sheep of Jesus. They can only dress as sheep. "Clothing" means just that "clothing." If you take a wolf and clothe the wolf with some lamb's skin, there is still a wolf under that lamb's skin. Jesus in His wisdom knew this. Therefore, He said false prophets will come in sheep's clothing. However, underneath the sheep's clothing is "ferocious wolves." This compliments Revelation 13:11.

The beast that "spoke like a dragon" also "had two horns like a lamb." That is, this lizard or dragon was dressed in sheep's clothing—he was clothed with two lamb's horns. However, internally, he is still a dragon. He spoke as a dragon; and Jesus said, out of the abundance of the heart the mouth speaks. The point is this: Christians must be able to see the spirits and hearts of men/women in the manner God sees the hearts and not concentrate on outward appearance. Hear God's word to Samuel concerning choosing a king of Israel: "Do not consider his appearance or his height, for I have rejected him. The LORD does not look at the things man looks at. Man looks at the outward appearance, but the LORD looks at the heart" (I Samuel 16:7).

THE WORD JUDGES.... THE HEART

*Hebrews 4:12, NIV: For **the word of God** is living and active. Sharper than any double-edged sword, **it** penetrates even to dividing soul and spirit, joints, and marrow; **it** judges the thoughts and attitudes of the heart.*

How will the disciples know those God did not approved? The Text above says "the word of God…. judges the thoughts and attitudes of the heart." The verse said the Word of God also "penetrates." In the next verse (Hebrews 4:13) it says, "Nothing in all creation is hidden from God's sight. Everything is uncovered and lain bare before the eyes of him to whom we must give account." This verse, which is a continuation of Hebrews 4:12t, calls "the word of God" "God's sight."

Therefore, the Word of God is also the eyes of God. I will now make a simple statement that may revolutionize your life. Since the Word of God is the sight of God, then, if His disciples put the Word of God in their hearts, then, consequently His disciples' eyes through God's Word will also penetrate "even to dividing soul and spirit, joints and marrow" and judge "the thoughts and attitudes of the heart." Yes! Yes! Yes! God's word can discern "spirit," even the spirit of the false prophet (compare 1 Corinthians 12:10, where one of the gifts of the Holy Spirit is "the discerning of spirits" (God's Spirit, man's spirit, and angels (chosen angels and satanic angels)).

This knowledge, beloved should encourage you to study and muse on the Word of God in conjunction with His Holy Spirit. God's Word "penetrates." His Word is so sharp and keen it "judges the thoughts and attitudes of the heart" and it is "dividing soul and spirit." This brings me to my next points. We must use the Word of God to see the spirit of the false ones (1 John 4:1). In Jesus' terms we must "watch for false prophets … **inwardly**" (Matthew 7:15). This is one of the ways to recognize false prophets. They may have sheep's clothing of lamb's horn (or lamb's power); however, their spirit may be unclean; dragon-like and/or frog-like (Revelation 13:11; 16:13).

DO NOT BELIEVE EVERY SPIRIT

*1 John 4:1, NIV: Dear friends, **do not believe every spirit,** but **test the spirits** to see whether they are from God, because many false prophets have gone out into the world.*

The command by the same apostle, John, the beloved, who saw the beast in Revelation 13:11 is: "do not believe every spirit." He said we should "test the spirits." John did not stop there. He linked "the spirits" to "many false prophets."

This is important to know, and with that said, let us look at the verse above considering all that was said in the previous paragraphs. First, let us remember what Jesus said to the disciples. He said, "Watch out for false prophets. They come to you in sheep's clothing, but inwardly they are ferocious wolves" (Matthew 7:15).

Jesus said the way to know false prophets is to understand that "inwardly" they are wolves. I previously indicated, "a person may clothe a wolf with sheep's clothing, but there is still a wolf under the clothes." I learned this from Jesus' statement in Matthew 7:15. The false prophets may look like sheep, however, "inwardly" (their "spirits") they are really wolves, or dragons.

Let us compare everything together (1 Corinthians 2:13). In Revelation 13: 11 John said that "another beast" had two horns like a lamb. However, "he <u>spoke</u> like a dragon." Our Lord said, "The good man brings good things out of the good stored up in his heart, and the evil man brings evil things out of the evil stored up in his heart. **For out of the overflow of his heart his mouth speaks"** (Luke 6:45). The beast may have lamb-like horns, but his mouth tells on him. He spoke like a dragon "out of the overflow of his heart." Jesus said the "mouth" reveals the "good" or "evil" that is in the "heart" as one "speaks."

Thus, this beast that looked like a lamb outwardly is really a dragon inwardly. John called this "inward part" of a person "spirit." Therefore, John said do not believe every spirit. We are to "test the spirits." How do we test? As we learned earlier, the Word of God, which is the eyes of God, divides "soul and spirit." There is also another important Person involved in seeing/exposing the antichrist spirits.

1 Corinthians 12:7, NIV: Now to each one the manifestation of the Spirit is given for the common good... **to another distinguishing between spirits.**

The Person of the Holy Spirit also extends a "service" (1 Corinthians 12:5) of distinguishing between spirits. This, beloved, is the love of God for His Church. He has given us His Holy Spirit to distinguish between spirits "for the common good." He always wants good for us, not evil. Therefore, He will expose all that will not do us "good." He is the Holy (Clean) Spirit. Therefore, He exposes all the dirty, or unclean spirits, the dragon, the false prophet, and the beast (Revelation 16:13-14). Note: there are nine gifts of the Spirit listed in 1 Corinthians 12:8-11, and there are nine fruit of the Spirit listed in Galatians 5. The fruit of the Spirit that correspond with the gift of "distinguishing between spirits" is the fruit of "faith."

The fruit of faith is seventh in line of the nine facets of the fruit of the Spirit and, the gift of distinguishing between spirits is also seventh in line of the gifts listed in 1 Corinthians 12:8-11. The point is this: As the Clean Spirit of God distinguishes between spirits, you must have the fruit of faith working. Because some of the spirits the Spirit of Jesus will show you in people/outside of people will be so unexpected that you will need the fruit of faith to believe it and to also believe that God can deliver the deceived who may be captivated by false spirits.

In other words, there are false brethren, false prophets, false apostles, false pastors, false Christs, etc. who claim to be of Jesus, the Christ; but they have a spirit which is not of God; and God wants His people to discern the difference. John also made another statement concerning recognition and/or distinguishing of the Clean Spirit and the wrong spirit. He said:

*1 John 4:2-3, NIV: ²This is how you can recognize the Spirit of God: Every **spirit** that acknowledges that Jesus Christ has come in the flesh is from God, ³but **every spirit that does not acknowledge Jesus is not from God.** This is the spirit of the antichrist, which you have heard is coming and even now is already in the world.*

The word "acknowledges" is a Greek compound that means "to say the same thing." In the context of this verse, "acknowledges" means the spirits of the prophets must "say the same thing" their "outward appearance" is saying about Jesus coming in the flesh. And false prophets' spirits must say the same thing their mouths are saying. In other words, prophet who uses words to say they believe that "Jesus Christ has come in the flesh" is not necessarily a disciple, if their **spirit** is not saying the same thing." That is, every spirit has a sound or a voice. Jesus said, "The **wind (lit., spirit)** blows wherever it pleases. You hear its **sound (lit., voice)** … (John 3:8a).

The apostle James also gave an interesting insight into the world of the demonic relative to their believing God is, yet they are considered unclean. In other words, a false prophet confessing an apparent belief in God with his mouth, does not necessarily means his spirit is clean or of God. James 2:19 says, *"You believe that there is one God. Good! Even the demons believe that — and shudder."* Demons believe, but they are "unclean spirits." So, false prophets confessing belief alone with their mouth is not enough. The spirit of a prophet must also confess what the mouth is saying. Paul, a true apostle, declared and demonstrated that he served the Lord with his mouth <u>and</u> spirit.

*Romans 1:9, NIV: God, whom **I serve with my whole heart (lit.; my spirit)** in preaching the gospel of his Son ….*

*Romans 1:9, KJV: For God is my witness, **whom I serve with my spirit** in the gospel of his Son ….*

*Romans 1:9, NASU: For God, **whom I serve in my spirit** in the preaching of the gospel of His Son ….*

Paul's spirit served the Lord **along with** his "verbal" confession of "preaching". That is, a person's mouth, or a person who acts religious (religious vocabulary, religious look, etc.), should not be saying he/she believes, yet the spirit in him/her is serving someone else (the false prophet). Nor should he/she who has a dirty spirit be acting as if he/she is a follower of Christ. The Church must realize that there is a real "spirit of antichrist;" and according to the Holy Writ, the spirit of antichrist is not the leopard beast in the book of Revelation. The spirit of antichrists are false prophets; and those who leave Jesus to follow seducing spirits.

*1 John 4:1-3: [1]Dear friends, do not believe every spirit, **but test the spirits** to see whether they are from God, **because many false prophets** have gone out into the world. [2]This is how you can recognize the Spirit of God: Every **spirit that** acknowledges that Jesus Christ has come in the flesh is from God, [3]but every spirit that does not acknowledge Jesus is not from God. **This is the spirit of the*** *antichrist, which you have heard is coming and even now is already in the world.*

If a prophet does not have the Spirit of God, he/she has the spirit of antichrist, also called the "false prophet", also called "another beast." We must not believe every spirit. Jesus said words are also spirit (John 6:63). The "another beast," in Revelation 13:11, "spoke like a dragon." This means out of his mouth precedes a spirit from within to deceive and recruit people for the beast's army. John brought this out in Revelation.

Revelation 16:12-14, NIV: [12]*The sixth angel poured out his bowl on the great river Euphrates, and its water was dried up to prepare the way for the kings from the East.* [13]*Then I saw **three evil spirits** that looked like frogs; they came **out of the mouth of the dragon,** out of the **mouth of the beast** and **out of the mouth of the false prophet**.* [14]*They are spirits of demons performing miraculous signs, and they go out to the kings of the whole world, to gather them for the battle on the great day of God Almighty.*

In the verses above John said, "I saw three evil spirits that looked like frogs." **One of them "came out of … the mouth of the false prophet."** 1 John 4:1 says, **"do not believe every spirit … <u>because many false prophets have gone out into the world.</u>"** John called the "every spirit" "many false prophets." In Revelation 16:13, the same thing is said another way. The false prophet had an "evil (Greek; unclean) spirit" come out of his mouth.

The false prophet is also a spirit, and a spirit also came out of his mouth, just as, the dragon is a spirit, and a spirit came out of his mouth. This <u>one</u> spirit, the false prophet, controls the "many false prophets." There is more. The spirit from the false prophet also performs "miraculous signs."

This is part of the sheep's clothing. Allow me to explain. The clothing of a sheep, including the male sheep, is their wool and their horns. The wool or sheepskin is for covering (Hebrews 11:37). One of the symbols of horns is power and authority.

*Deuteronomy 33:17, NIV: In majesty he is like a firstborn bull; his horns are **the horns** of a wild ox. **With them** he will gore (lit., butt with horns) the nations, even those at the ends of the earth. Such are the ten thousand of Ephraim; such are the thousands of Manasseh.*

*Daniel 8:5-8, NIV: ⁵As I was thinking about this, suddenly a goat with **a prominent horn** between his eyes came from the west, crossing the whole earth without touching the ground. ⁶He came toward **the two-horned ram** I had seen standing beside the canal and charged at him in great rage. ⁷I **saw him attack the ram furiously, striking the ram and shattering his two horns**. The ram was powerless to stand against him; the goat knocked him to the ground and trampled on him, and none could rescue the ram from his power.*

The authority of a male goat or a ram is gained using the power or strength of his horn (Daniel 8). He uses it to fight for leadership within the flock. In fact, in Deuteronomy 33:17, the word "gore" means to "butt with horns," "to war against." The true Lamb of God has seven horns. "Seven," in the Hebrew language, means "complete," "rest" and "oath." Therefore, the Lamb of God, Jesus, has rested in the Holy Spirit complete or all power and authority (Matthew 28:17) that was established by "resting" in God's "oath" (Hebrews 6:17).

Jesus "butted" the Devil with His "seven horns." The prince of this world (Satan) is judged (John 16:11)! Horns are symbols of power. Thus, the two horns of the false prophet are representative of the limited miraculous power of its unclean spirit that it functions in. These lying signs of this satanic spirit are part of the false prophet's clothing (2 Thessalonians 2:9-11; Matthew 24:24, etc.). His clothing of the miraculous signs is part of his cloak to seduce (Revelation 13:18).

I would like to give a word of balance at this point. The statement above is not saying that all miracles are not of God. God performs miracles (Acts 3:1-8; Acts 5; Acts 11:28, Acts 13: 8-12; Acts 14:6-11; Hebrews 2:4). And on the other hand, John the Baptist—the Elijah Ministry—did no "sign" (John 10:41). Therefore, an absence of power in a real man of God, does not mean that God is not with that man of God.

HORNS OF POWER

*Revelation 5:6, NIV: Then I saw a Lamb, looking as if it had been slain, standing in the center of the throne, encircled by the four living creatures and the elders. He had **seven horns** and seven eyes, which **are the seven spirits of God** sent out into all the earth.*

Now note: The "seven horns… are the seven spirits of God." (1) The Spirit of the Lord, (2) the Spirit of Wisdom, (3) the Spirit of Understanding, (4) the Spirit of Counsel, (5) the Spirit of Power, (6) the Spirit of Knowledge and (7) the Spirit of the fear of the Lord (Isaiah 11:2). There are not seven separate Holy Spirits (Ephesians 4:3-6). However, there are seven manifestations of His Spirit, which means the Holy Spirit has no measure or limit (John 3:34; Revelation 1:4; 3:1, 4:5; 5:6).

In Revelation 13:11, the false prophet also had two horns. These two horns also mean that he operated through false witness (two) of the manifestation of his lying spirit. One manifestation is the spirit of the image of the beast that causes the image to speak and kill (Revelation 13:15); another witness is the evil frog-like spirit that worked unclean "miraculous signs" (Revelation 16:12-14). That is, the false prophet also could cause fire to come down from heaven to the earth in the sight of men (Revelation 13:13-14). Satan did the same thing in the book of Job (Job 1:12 w/Job 1:16).

One must be careful to discern what kind of "horns" are performing the miracles he/she follows. Are the miracles from

God gathering you to the Lamb of God? Or are the signs from the spirits of the three beasts (the dragon, the beast, and false prophet, alias, "another beast") gathering you against God, "into the battle of that great day of God Almighty." Are you being gathered "into" the "place" (a spiritual place) called "Armageddon" — mountain of the gathering, mountain of the crowd, or mountain "to cut off"[1] (Revelation 16:14-16)?

Discern who you are "gathering" with and the "crowd" that you partake of. Is there a "voice" or a false sign urging you to worship the dragon, or to worship the beast (government systems), or worshipping of a man or woman (ranging from false preachers to athletes and celebrities), or an idol, or demons, or manmade objects, etc. instead of Jesus, the Christ?   There is a gathering happening in the earth against the Lord and His Christ. And the Scriptures prewrote that the false prophet along with the dragon and the beast will especially target people who participate in "disfigured-togetherness" — primarily those who "God" gives over to practice same-sexuality, bisexuality, sexual changes by mutilating their bodies, anal sex either males or females, bestiality, etc. (Revelation 16:15 w/Romans 1:27 in the context of Romans 1:18-32). These are spirits of devils causing a gathering "into the battle" against Jesus, the King of kings and the Lord of Lords (1 Timothy 4:1-2 with Revelation 16:13-16; Revelation 19:19-20).

One must "test" the spirits of leaders. There is a difference between testing and judging. The Spirit of Jesus Christ (Philippians 1:19) will bring salvation. The spirit of antichrist causes a person to leave God and follow the deceived crowd; follow the beast and his/its image (including the things of the

---

[1] These definitions are per Fausset's Bible Dictionary definition of the root word for "Megiddo." It is also noteworthy to point out that no such mountain (Armageddon) exists in the natural.

world), and so on (1 John 4:6; 1 John 2:15; 1 Corinthians 7:31; Revelation 13).

WHO IS THE ANTICHRIST?

*1 John 4:1-3, NIV: ¹Dear friends, do not believe every spirit, but **test**² the spirits to see whether they are from God, because many false prophets have gone out into the world. ²This is how you can recognize the Spirit of God: Every spirit that acknowledges that Jesus Christ has come in the flesh is from God, ³but every spirit that does not acknowledge Jesus is not from God. This is the spirit of the antichrist, which you have heard is coming and even now is already in the world.*

1 John 2:18-19, NIV: ¹⁸Dear children, this is the last hour; and as you have heard that the antichrist is coming, even now many antichrists have come. This is how we know it is the last hour. ¹⁹ They went out from us, but they did not really belong to us. For if they had belonged to us, they would have remained with us; but their going showed that none of them belonged to us.

For many generations, after the death of the first apostles, men have taught that the antichrist is the beast to come. This trend began in the 1500s. However, what some have overlooked is that in every age antichrist exists. "The beast" of Revelation 13:2 or, the "man of lawlessness" in 2 Thessalonians 2:3 is not the only facet of the antichrist. The antichrist consists of the "many false prophets" and those who turn back from following Christ Jesus. Let us examine this truth.

John said believe not every spirit. He then called the "every spirit" he referenced "many false prophets." He did not stop there. He continued by calling the spirit of the false prophets "the

---

² "Test" is the Greek word "dokimazo," from the root "dokeo" defined as "seem" which means an impression of being and/or that which appears to the observation of understanding, it also means to give an estimate of someone or something, an opinion.

spirit of antichrist." These false prophets may look like they belong to the Christ; however, do not be deceived by them. They are "antichrist," with an understanding that "anti" means "instead of, in place of, or against." Antichrist is the spirit, the false prophet, or the false prophet of the book of Revelation, or any false prophet who dresses like he is a sheep of Jesus. This antichrist's purpose is to seduce the saints from following and "abiding" in the Lord Jesus Christ, the Son of the living God. How will he/she do this? By false prophesies, by false signs, and false miracles, false wonders, sheep's clothing, and so on. Thus, the seduced also becomes antichrist (1 John 2:19).

*1 John 4:3, NIV: But **every spirit** that does not acknowledge Jesus is not from God. **This is the spirit of the antichrist,** which you have heard is coming and **even now is already in the world.***

An important point is this: "the antichrist… even now is **already** in the world." Paul also said, *"For the secret power of lawlessness is **already** at work; but the one who now holds it back will continue to do so till he is 'becomes' out of the 'middle'"* (2 Thessalonians 2:7). *"Dear children, this is the last hour; and as you have heard that the antichrist is coming, **even now** many antichrists **have** come. This is how we know it is the last hour"* (1 John 2:18). These verses explicitly state that the antichrist **is not** totally futuristic.

The antichrist exists "even now." For emphasis, the antichrist is a spirit that "is already at work." Therefore, stop looking for the antichrist to come. It/he/she/they are already here, as we will see in a moment. The next point is this. According to 1 John, the antichrist is a spirit that speaks through false prophets (1 John 4:1). In other words, the antichrist is the "many false prophets." There is also another facet of the antichrist that is serious. Antichrist is any person who stops following the Christ.

1 John 2:18-19, NIV: ¹⁸Dear children, this is the last hour; and as you have heard that the antichrist is coming, even now many antichrists have come. This is how we know it is the last hour. [19]**They went out from us, but they did not really belong to us.** *For if they had belonged to us, they would have remained with us; but their going showed that none of them belonged to us.*

Antichrists are those who "went out from us." This knowledge should stop people from so easily going back on God or falling away from the Lord Jesus. Those who have not endured and "remained with us" are antichrist. The heavy part about this is that "they did not really belong to us." Anyone who denies Christ after knowing Jesus is considered an antichrist. Therefore, they did not really belong to us. The Bible calls them liars. Their actions state "a lie" by saying that Jesus is not the Christ when they turn their backs on Him.

The beloved John said, *"Who is the liar? It is the man who denies (or contradicts) that Jesus is the Christ"* (1 John 2:22). They are crucifying Jesus again (Revelation 11:8, Hebrews 6:6). Such a man/woman is the antichrist— "he denies the Father and the Son" (1 John 2:22). Any former followers of Christ who embrace another religion and deny Christ Jesus are antichrists. Do not trust the other religion who pose another way to God, other than Jesus, the Way; they are liars (John 2:24-25). They are false prophets.

The false prophet of Revelation 13:11 will apparently manifest is a beast man and is "another beast" spirit behind every false religion, and he likes to seduce followers of Christ out of their belief in Jesus. The false prophet's main target is to try to deceive the "elect" of God (Matthews 24:24). Remember, "No one who denies the Son has the Father" (1 John 2:23).

Anyone who claims they are serving the same God as Christians, but denies Jesus Christ as being the Son of God is an antichrist.

The scripture quoted above says that if they deny Jesus as the Christ, then they are not serving the same "Father." Another aspect of the antichrist is the fact that he/she denies Jesus "as coming in the flesh."

*2 John 1:7, NIV: Many **deceivers,** who do not acknowledge Jesus Christ **as coming in the flesh,** have gone out into the world. Any such person is the deceiver and the antichrist.*

*2 John 1:7, KJV: For many **deceivers** are entered into the world, **who confess not that Jesus Christ is come in the flesh**. This is a deceiver and an antichrist.*

The antichrists are those who do not acknowledge that, "Jesus Christ **is** come in the flesh." The little word "is" emphasizes present tense. There are many people who refuse to believe that Jesus is the Son of God who came in the flesh. "And without controversy great is the mystery of godliness: God was manifest in the flesh, justified in the Spirit, seen of angels, preached unto the Gentiles, believed on in the world, received up into glory" (1 Timothy 3:16, KJV).

Jesus, the Christ did come in the flesh, He died on the cross, and He is resurrected and is living at/in/out of the right hand of God; and He is still coming in the flesh. Jesus in His omnipresence is also living in the Body (flesh[3]) of His Church.

The antichrists are those who refuse to believe that Jesus is living in us—the Church. Jesus Christ is come in the flesh. That is, He is **also** come in flesh of the Church. Jesus is not millions of miles away in space somewhere. He is here in His people. The Holy Writ says, *"To them [Saints] God has chosen to make known among the Gentiles the glorious riches of this mystery, which is Christ **in** you, the hope of glory" (Colossians 1:27).* The "Spirit of Jesus" is in us **now!**

---

[3] This "flesh" is not referring to the sinful flesh nature.

1 Corinthians 3:16, NIV: Don't you know that you yourselves are God's temple and that God's Spirit dwells in your midst?

1 Corinthians 3:16, NASB: Do you not know that you are a temple of God and that the Spirit of God dwells in you.

*Acts 16:7, NIV: And after they came to Mysia, they were trying to go into Bithynia, and **the Spirit of Jesus** did not allow them.*

*Acts 16:7, NASB: And after they came to Mysia, they were trying to go into Bithynia, and **the Spirit of Jesus** did not allow them.*

*Romans 8:9, NIV: "And if **anyone does not have the Spirit of Christ,** he does not belong to Christ."*

All who deny that Jesus is living in the flesh of His Church "<u>now</u>" is antichrist. They do "not belong to Christ." Therefore, watch those pseudo saints and so-called prophets who have a doctrine that denies that Jesus is come in the flesh.

That is, some say Jesus is in their lives, yet they live a life of ungodliness. He came literally approximately 2000 years ago, and, in Spirit, He is come in us presently. An application of this denial of Jesus' Spirit coming in the flesh is the one who says, "The Holy Spirit manifesting in our body by the evidence of speaking in tongues is evil, or demonic." I guess they have not read Mark 3:28-30, especially verses 29 and 30 of Mark 3.

Mark 3:28-30 teach that anyone who says that the work being done by the Holy Sprit is unclean or demonic is saying an unpardonable sin (The oldest Greek text for Mark 3:29 reads: "eternal sin" as can be seen in the New International Version and the New American Standard — Updated Edition). There are many false brethren and false prophets among the saints. They like Jannes and Jambres, the two sorcerers who opposed Moses, are resisting the truth of the power of God. But they will go no further. They only have limited power.

A VISION FROM THE LORD JESUS CHRIST

Early 1990s; a morning—between 3-5 AM. Judy and I were in a season of intensified prayer. On that day, we prayed through the night. After the intensified prayer, we laid down to get some sleep; however, immediately I was in a vision. In the vision, I saw a red (komodo-like) dragon and I in the heat of a battle. I could see that I wrestled this red dragon out of the sky to the ground. I then descended from the heavenly sphere to see what became of the dragon. I could see that my clothes were ripped up as a result of being engaged in intensified battle against this red dragon. As I was descending, the red dragon began to pursue me, again. I ascended again to the heavens as he pursued me.

As he was pursuing me, I turned toward him to fight, and fire came out of my mouth and devoured him (Compare Revelation 11:5, Jeremiah 23:29). As a result of the fire that came out of my mouth, the beast then fell, again, to the ground as dead, however he was not. As I descended from the heavenly, I saw my wife walking towards the now fallen beast to throw on it some sort of solid foam. In the vision, my wife was strong in appearance; and the plats of her hair was long, thick, and sturdy in appearance. As she was about to approach the dragon to assess the condition of the red dragon, I called out to her and said, "He is not dead as he may appear."

As I said this to my wife, the beast stood up; and I could see him in plain view. To my amazement, though, the red dragon had mutated into an animal-man; that is, his appearance was that of a man (he resembled a very prominent televangelist prophet), but he had two huge horns like a male lamb. The horns started from his temple curling back towards his ears, as the appearance of a ram with great horns. At this sight, the vision ended.

As previously indicated, Revelation 13:11 describes "another beast" that has two horns like a lamb; however, it speaks like a dragon. This same "another beast" is also called "the false prophet" in Revelation 16:13 and Revelation 19:20. It is also worthy to note that Satan is called a fiery red dragon; hence this "another beast" that speaks "as" a dragon is a dragon. "As," in Revelation 13:11, is the Greek word "hos" which is defined as "who," "which," "what," and "that." Hence, "he 'who' is a dragon," speaks "what", "as a dragon."

THE FIERY RED DRAGON'S TAIL

Revelation 12:3-4, NIV: ³Then another sign appeared in heaven: an enormous **red dragon** *with seven heads and ten horns and seven crowns on his heads.* ⁴**His tail** *swept a third of the* **stars out of the sky (lit., heaven)** *and flung them to the earth. The dragon stood in front of the woman who was about to give birth, so that he might devour her child the moment it was born.*

The red dragon is the original serpent, called the Devil and Satan (Revelation 12:9). The fiery red dragon in the book of Revelation used his tail to throw a third part of the stars of heaven to the earth. This dragon is a corporate entity. His seven heads are seven ruling angels and/or visible or invisible kings who dominate some so called "elders" and "prominent men." The dragon's "tail" is a metaphor for the "many false prophets." This is seen in God's statement through Isaiah.

Isaiah 9:15, NIV: The elders and prominent men are the head, **the prophets who teach lies are the tail.**

This is a revealing statement. **"Prophets who teach lies are the tail."** "Lies" or "the lie" ranges from telling a lie, idol worship, demon worship, satanic worship, dragon worship, animal worship, man worship, beast worship, the lie of world government ("kosmoskratos") worship, false prophets who state that God has said something which God has not spoken, sexual perversion, denying or contradicting that Jesus is the Christ, the Son of God, the lie of "another gospel" that equates prosperity (worldly success, "being over much," money or riches) with godliness or salvation, and so on.

Jesus also says that false believers and false leaders have a liar for their father. Jesus said, *"You belong to your father, the devil… for he is a liar and the father of lies" (John 8:44).* The Devil is a liar and the father of lies. Therefore, ministers that "teach lies" are fathered by Satan. Do you see the connection? Metaphorically, the teachers who teach lies are the "tail." What tail? The tail of the dragon! There was a great man who had to deal with a serpent's tail; his name is Moses.

Moses had to take up a "snake" by the "tail." In the New Testament, the word "dragon" used in the book of Revelation means "a large serpent" (See Vines Dictionary). Thus, what Moses did with the serpent's tail points to the fact that he would take the dragons of Egypt by their tails. It is the same way in this generation. In fact, Moses's rod did indeed turn into a dragon that consumed two dragons that the sorcerers of Egypt manifested in the presence of Moses and Aaron.

The apostles and prophets of God must take the dragon by the tail to stop its lies. We must stop it from throwing down the stars — saints — to the ground with its lies. Note" "stars of heaven" are used symbolically to referenced saints as seen in these verses: Genesis 37:9-10; Daniel 12:3; Matthew 2:1-2; Philippians 2:14-15).

MOSES AND THE SERPENT'S TAIL

Exodus 4:2-5, NIV: ² *Then the LORD said to him, "What is that in your hand?" "A staff," he replied.* ³ *The LORD said, "Throw it on the ground." Moses threw it on the ground, and it became a snake, and he ran from it.* ⁴ **Then the LORD said to him,** *"Reach out your hand and* **take it by the tail."** *So, Moses reached out and took hold of the snake and it turned back into a staff in his hand.* ⁵ *"This," said the LORD, "is so that they may believe that the LORD, the God of their fathers — the God of Abraham, the God of Isaac and the God of Jacob — has appeared to you."*

Moses was empowered by our LORD to go into Egypt and deliver the people of God. God knew he was destined to encounter some of the false powers of Egypt. Therefore, God prepared him. Moses had some concerns about the people's beliefs in the fact that God had indeed sent him. In the process of God strengthening Moses. God empowered Moses to take the "snake" by the "tail." That is, God turned Moses' staff into a "snake." He then commanded Moses to take up the snake by the "tail."

Principle: In these days those who can take the dragon by his tail will validate their ministry that the Head of the Church has sent them to deliver the ethnics out of the holds of principalities and authorities in the heavenlies (Exodus 4:5, Ephesians 3, Ephesians 6).

As we learned earlier in this chapter, the tail of the snake is emblematic of the false prophets. In Moses' case, the tail of the serpent was symbolic of the sorcerers (false prophets) of Egypt—a type of the world. The Hebrew for "snake" means, a snake from its hiss; to whisper a (magic) spell; to prognosticate; divine, enchanter, (use) enchantment, etc. (Strong's Concordance # 5175 & 5172).

Thus, the snake points to the enchanters of Egypt who Moses would defeat. It is Moses' encounter with the sorcerers/false prophets of Egypt I will use to show the limited power of the dragon's tail. In addition, before I discuss this "limited power," I will show how in this age there is a present application of Moses' encounter with the "tail" of the serpent. Peter talked about being "established in the present truth" (2 Peter 1:12, KJV). All the truths of the Bible can be applied to our present season. We are presently in the "terrible times in the last days." However, like Moses, we will know the "ways" of God which will enable us to function in the "works" of God.

2 Timothy 3:1-9, NIV: ¹But mark this: There will be terrible times in the last days.² People will be lovers of themselves, lovers of money, boastful, *proud, abusive, disobedient to their parents, ungrateful, unholy, ³without love, unforgiving, **slanderous (lit., devils)**, without self-control, brutal, not lovers of the good, ⁴ treacherous, rash, conceited, lovers of pleasure rather than lovers of God— ⁵ having a form of godliness but denying its power. Have nothing to do with them.⁶ They are the kind who worm their way into homes and gain control over weak-willed women, who are loaded down with sins and are swayed by all kinds of evil desires, ⁷ always learning but never able to acknowledge the truth. ⁸ Just as Jannes and Jambres opposed Moses, so also these men oppose the truth — men of depraved minds, who, as far as the faith is concerned, are rejected. ⁹ But they will not get very far because, as in the case of those men, their folly will be clear to everyone.*

Paul said, "Mark this: There will be terrible times in the last days." There is a mark that distinguishes the terrible times in the last days. There is a "mark" that will be "in" the "last days." Another way of saying it is: The last days will be marked or recognized by certain prevailing attitudes.

"People will be lovers of themselves." Some of them the Scripture defines as "devils." Does this describe the world and some in the Church today? People will be "lovers of money, boastful, proud, abusive," etc. Sounds like this age, doesn't it? There is also another mark of the last days, children being "disobedient to their parents ("parents" is masculine in the Greek, therefore the word relates to children being disobedient to fathers)." Does this describe the world today? The list goes on: "lovers of pleasure rather than lovers of God" (Contrast Hebrews 11:24-25). You and I both know that the list given by the apostle describes this age exactly. That means that we are "in the last days."

Paul called these days "terrible times." He did not stop there. He said, "Have nothing to do with them." Why was the beloved apostle so harsh? It appears that he is describing most people in the world. Therefore, who can be saved—Matthew 19:25-26—if we are to "have nothing to do with them?"

The understanding is: he compared these people to Jannes and Jambres who were Egypt's sorcerers that withstood Moses. The Scripture says, **"Just as** Jannes and Jambres opposed Moses …" (2 Timothy 3:8). The attitudes that Paul lists, spring out of sorcery, highly developed enchanters, witchcraft, wizardry, necromancy, divination, and through those who have familiar spirits, those who are practicing psychics and warlocks, etc. According to the book of Deuteronomy, we are commanded not to associate with people who practices these things (Deuteronomy 18:9-14).

 This is why the Spirit of Jesus through Paul was so assertive — "have nothing to do with them." There is a dark power behind the attitudes Paul listed above. In other words, the same attitude that the sorcerers of that age displayed against Moses is the same attitude false prophets of this age has against God and His saints; and it is manifested through all who have contact with the lawless powers like that of the two sorcerers of Egypt.

This truth also shows the lifestyles that people live in secret. The attitudes that Paul lists stem out of contacts with sorcerers. In other words, the reason why these attitudes are treated so harshly by Paul is because they stem from the secret art of sorcery and contact with any form of the secret sects of this present darkness. Let us now see how sorcerers — the serpent's tail (Jannes and Jambres) of Pharaoh — were defeated by Moses. I will begin by reviewing an interpretation of the "two horns" that was discussed in Chapter 1.

"Then I saw another beast, coming out of the earth. He had two horns like a lamb, but he spoke like a dragon" (Revelation 13:11, NIV). Remember the true Lamb of God has seven horns (Revelation 5). Seven in the Hebrew means "complete," "rest," and "oath" (See Strong's Concordance). Therefore, Jesus has complete power and

authority (Matthew 28:18). It follows that the beast of Revelation 13: 11 has limited power to his false witness—he only has two horns.

Therefore, one of the applications of the two horns is this: they are symbolic of limited power—the limited power of the Devil. The power of the devil is limited when it comes to dealing with the people of God. (John 14:30; Colossians 1:13; Job 1:12; Job 2:6). However, for those who deny the truth (Jesus), God will allow "the working of Satan with all power and signs and lying wonders" to deceive all who reject the "love of the Truth"—personified in Jesus (See 2 Thessalonians 2:1-12).

The New International Version says Satan will display "all kinds of counterfeit miracles, signs and wonders." However, when it comes to the saints who love and believe the truth, the powers of darkness are limited. The false prophets only have two horns, not seven.; thus, the powers of diviners or all counterfeit prophet in the world are limited in their scope relative to true believers. The powers of Egypt that Moses defeated are also limited. God alone has all power in heaven and earth.

LIMITED POWERS OF EGYPT

Exodus 7:8-9, NIV: [8]The LORD said to Moses and Aaron, [9]"When Pharaoh says to you, 'Perform a miracle, 'then say to Aaron, 'Take your staff and throw it down before Pharaoh,' and it will become a snake.

The Lord asked Moses and Aaron to do the same thing with this staff that Moses had done with God on the mountain— "throw it down before Pharaoh, and it will become a **snake.**" This time (Exodus 7:9) the Hebrew meaning of the word "snake" is not the same as the first time God asked Moses to lay down his staff. The Hebrew word for "snake" in this instance is (tanniyn, or tanniym—Strong's Old Testament: #8577) is not the same word for "snake" in Exodus 4:3 (nachash, Strong's Old Testament:

#5175). The word snake in Exodus 7:9 is also translated as "dragon" in the King James Version.

*Ezekiel 29:3, KJV: Speak, and say, thus says the Lord GOD; Behold, I am against you, Pharaoh king of Egypt, the great **dragon (Hebrew, tanniyn, or tanniym)** that lies in the midst of his rivers, which has said, my river is mine own, and I have made it for myself.*

*Isaiah 27:1, KJV: In that day, the LORD with his sore and great and strong sword shall punish leviathan the piercing serpent, even leviathan that crooked serpent; and he shall slay the **dragon (Hebrew, tanniyn, or tanniym)** that is in the sea.*

In other words, the first time Moses threw his staff down it became a serpent. The second time the staff became a dragon. The first time Moses picked up the serpent by the tail. This time Moses will again pick up the dragons of Egypt by the tail, except, in a different way. Moses will use the unmatchable power of God to take the two representatives of Egypt by their "tails." In modern vernacular, Moses is going to "kick some tail," as we will discuss in a moment. Yes! Yes! Yes! The Church will also kick the dragon's tail. Let us see how this will be accomplished. It follows that after Aaron's threw down Moses' staff by the command of Moses, the rod turned into the dragon (Exodus 7:10); however, Pharaoh's sorcerers did the same.

*Exodus 7:11-12, NIV: [11]Pharaoh then summoned wise men and sorcerers, and **the Egyptian magicians also did the same things** by their secret arts: [12] **Each one threw down his staff and it became a snake (lit; dragon). But Aaron's staff swallowed up their staffs.***

The sorcerers and magicians "also did the same thing." Except, they use the secret arts of the Devil. They used enchantment (King James Version).

Principle: In this age, there are some acts of God that false prophets will copy by the "secret power" or "secret arts" of the Devil (Revelation 13:12-13; Revelation 16:14; Deuteronomy 13:1-2; Revelation 13:15 with Genesis 2:7).

Now you can understand why John was so firm: *"Dear friends, do not believe every spirit, but test the spirits to see whether they are from God, because many false prophets have gone out into the world"* (1 John 4:1). Paul was even stronger than John. He said, *"Have nothing to do with them"* (2Timothy 3:5).

The fact that the magicians copied Moses was not the only thing that was stated. Moses and Aaron's staff eventually "swallowed up" the sorcerers' staffs. Remember, I said above that Aaron's staff (or Moses's staff that Aaron used) by Moses's command turned into a "dragon." I also said this fact is significant to know. The point is this. Aarons' staff that turned into a dragon swallowed up the two dragons of Egypt.

Thus, the unmatched ability of God's power is demonstrated in the fact that Aaron's staff swallowed up two crocodiles, not mere snakes. The sorcerers and magicians copied Moses' command. But their powers were limited. They could only copy. But the Almighty God's "all power" swallowed up their limited power. The two dragons of Egypt "experienced" firsthand the "tongue" of Aaron's rod (representative of God's "house"). Hear the scripture again: "But Aaron's staff swallowed up their staffs."

The snake in scripture is also symbolic of shrewdness. Jesus said, *"Be as shrewd as snakes and as innocent as doves"* (Matthews 10:16). The snakes of Egypt are also a metaphor of the "shrewdness" of the world. However, the wisdom of God will take the shrewdness of this world by the tail and swallow it up. The false prophets' wisdom of this world is limited. God took the snakes (crocodiles or dragons) of Egypt by their tails.

"Oh, the depth of the riches of the wisdom and knowledge of God! How

unsearchable his judgments, and his paths beyond tracing out! "Who has known the mind of the Lord? Or who has been his counselor" (Romans 11:33-34)? Jannes and Jambres must have been stunned. This was only the beginning of their demise. This was the first of three demonstrations by God that the power of the dragon's tail is limited and is swallowed up by Jesus.

COPYING IS LIMITED

2 Corinthians 11:13-15, NIV: [13]*For such men are* **false apostles,** *deceitful workmen,* **masquerading as apostles of Christ.** [14] *And no wonder, for Satan himself masquerades as an angel of light.* [15]*It is not surprising, then, if his servants masquerade as servants of righteousness. Their end will be what their actions deserve.*

Copying is one of Satan's deceptive ways, or one of the false prophet deceptive ways. Satan and is corporate Satan has appeared in many false prophets as "an angel of light," declaring an adulterated gospel. The Bible said not to listen to any "man" or "angel" who brings another gospel (Galatians 1:8-9). Fallen angels, especially Satan, bring false light or pseudo religion. "It is not surprising, then, if his servants masquerade as servants of righteousness."

Jannes and Jambres did the same thing against Moses. They also masquerade enchantment power[4] as God's power. That is, they masqueraded their power to appear to be a power from God (compare Acts 8:9-10). However, God only allowed it for three times—Exodus 7:12—snake; Exodus 7:21-22—blood and Exodus 8:6-7—frogs)—and that was it. God allowed the satanic power of the sorcerers to work for a season to deceive Pharaoh with the energy of error that his heart should be hardened.

---

[4] Enchantment is linked to the "soul of leviathan," a dragon of the sea that also prefigures Satan.

The Holy Writ says, *"And for this cause, **God shall send them** strong delusion (lit; energy of error), that they should believe a lie"* (2 Thessalonians 2:11, KJV). Why did God allow this? *"That they all might be damned who believed not the truth but had pleasure in unrighteousness"* (2 Thessalonians 2:12, KJV). The "truth" that Pharaoh did not believe was that our God is the only God (Exodus 5:2). Thus, God allowed this lying energy to work three times in order to harden Pharaoh's heart in his unbelief.

In Revelation 16: 13-14, it was "three" unclean spirits that were allowed to perform false miracles. This points to the fact that in the same way God allowed the false sorcerers and magicians of Egypt to be limited to three copies, the evil spirits that perform miracles are also limited to three—the dragon, the beast, and the false prophets (Revelation 16:13-14). The question must be asked then, why does God allow this falsehood to continue?

Principle: In this age it appears that the world's false prophets—psychics, the palm readers, necromancers, warlocks, sorcerers, Satan worshippers, wizards (male witches), witches, believers in the New Age Movement, false teachers in the Church, etc, can copy God's power and God's prophetic in a limited way. However, God will stymie the false ones.

HARD HEARTS

*Exodus 7:22, NIV: But the Egyptian magicians did the same things by their secret arts, and **Pharaoh's heart became hard;** he would not listen to Moses and Aaron, just as the LORD had said.*

*2 Thessalonians 2:8-9, Berean Literal Bible: ⁸And then the lawless one will be revealed, whom the Lord Jesus will consume with the breath of His mouth and will annul by the appearing of His coming, ⁹whose coming is according to the working of **Satan, in every power, and in signs, and in wonders of falsehood,** ¹⁰and in every deception of wickedness unto those perishing, in return for which they did not* *receive the love of the truth in order for them to be saved. ¹¹And because of this, **God** will send to them a working of delusion, for them to believe what is false, ¹²in order that all those not having believed the truth but having delighted in unrighteousness should be judged.*

In 2 Thessalonians 2:9-10 states that God will allow false miracles, false signs, and false wonders to occur. Why? It will be for those who have not believed the love of the truth—the love of Jesus, the Truth. Therefore, God will send "them a 'energy of error' to believe 'the lie'." Allow me to make the above statements practical.

God is allowing the false prophets of the world to perform their false miracles. False signs are being energized by the words of the false prophets. These false signs will harden the hearts of those who refuse to believe the truth of Jesus. The Devil through his fake agencies will cause people who listen to him to become hard against God; because they may believe the false power they experience is legitimate.

They are saying, "The things I am hearing in the world from the psychics and witches are coming to pass. Therefore, why should I follow Jesus? I can have the pleasures of the world and prophetic insight." Thus, their hearts are hardened, and the scripture—2 Thessalonians 2:11-12—is fulfilled.

God is allowing them to believe the "energy" of "the lie" that they may be "condemned," according to 2 Thessalonians 2:11-12. I plead with you. If you are involved with the psychics, witches, warlocks, palm-readers, etc., of this dark-age stop! Turn to God, and do not harden your heart. Receive the love of Jesus—Now! It is indeed possible to get victory out of most of the beast's system (Revelation 15:2).

God hardened Pharaoh's heart for a similar reason. It was after the sorcerer and magicians performed their false miracle that the

Holy Writ said that Pharaoh became harder in his heart. Listen to the scripture again: *"But the Egyptian magicians did the same things by their secret arts, and Pharaoh's heart became hard; he would not listen to Moses and Aaron, just as the LORD had said"* (Exodus 7:22).

Notice the conjunction "and." It connects the first and second statements in the scripture. God hardened Pharaoh's heart when he believed the secret arts (power) of the enchanters instead of the voice of God's power. The same thing will happen today if a person refuses God's power, God's truth, and God's love (2 Thessalonians 2: 10; 1 Corinthians 1:18 and 1:24, etc.) and chooses Satan's lies. Remember though, the power of sorcery is limited. There are things that our Lord Jesus Christ has reserved that nothing false can copy.

"THEY COULD NOT"

Exodus 8:16-18, NIV: *16Then the LORD said to Moses, "Tell Aaron, `Stretch out your staff and strike the dust of the ground,' and throughout the land of Egypt the dust will become gnats." 17 They did this, and when Aaron stretched out his hand with the staff and struck the dust of the ground, gnats came upon men and animals. All the dust throughout the land of Egypt became gnats. 18But when **the magicians tried** to produce gnats by their secret arts, **they could not**. And the gnats were on men and animals.*

God showed the magicians who is all-powerful. God is all-powerful! They tried to copy God for the fourth time, and "they could not." This "present evil age" (Galatians 1:4) will try to copy God's signs sent to judge. However, in the words of Paul, "they will not get very far" (2 Timothy 3:9). The powers of the false prophets are limited. They may reproduce for a while. But one day, all the false prophets of the world will acknowledge that God's finger is all-powerful.

The magicians said to Pharaoh, *"This is the finger of God"* (Exodus

8:19). Yes! Yes! Yes! Jesus said He cast out demons by the "finger of God" (Luke 11:20). Matthew's record calls the "finger of God" "the Spirit of God" (Matthews 12:28). God's Spirit power is limitless. The false prophet's spirit can only deceive those who are given over to believe the lie and "shameful-togetherness."

In Revelation 16: 13-14, the limited power of three evil (lit.; unclean) spirits performed false miracles. However, they could not defeat the all-power of Jesus (Revelation 19:20). Yes, one day, the world will acknowledge that The Holy[5] Spirit is all-powerful (Revelation 11:11-13; Philippians 2:10-11). "The Finger of God," which is the Holy or Pure Spirit of God, can do things that unclean spirits cannot do. "The Finger of God," through His true prophets and apostles, will take the dragon by his tail.

Make sure that it is the "Clean" Spirit of God who is doing the miracles and not "unclean" spirits (Compare Revelation 16:14). I reiterate: The fact that the magicians "could not" copy the act of producing lice showed that God, through Moses, had taken the two dragons of Egypt by the tail. The Lord God stymied the two "tails" of Egypt. Satan's power is limited. Do not allow the fake powers of false prophets to seduce you into following the darkness that exists in this age!

Understand that psychics, palm readers, necromancers, warlocks, sorcerers, Satan worshippers, wizards—male witches, witches, believers in the new age movement, false teachers in the Church who teach that capital equals godliness, etc., are limited in what they can do or say to a true disciple. They have an end. *"Their end will be what their actions deserve" (2 Corinthians 11:15b).* The "tail" of the dragon will be exposed for what it is—the many false prophets (2 Timothy 3:9).

---

[5] The Greek for "Holy" is "Hagios" which also means "Clean" or "Pure."

Now before I conclude, I will give a brief review of the other two acts of Moses that the false prophets of Egypt copied and show how the false ones of this dark age cause the same verdicts to trap this generation. Above I indicated that God only allowed the sorcerers to copy Moses for three times—Exodus 7:12—snake; Exodus 7:21-22—blood and Exodus 8:6-7—frogs)—and that was it. I covered the "snake" briefly. I will now canvass the "blood" and the "frog." The question is: "What is the principle behind the blood being reproduced by the false prophets of Egypt?" I will explain it this way. Moses produced blood that caused "death" and a "foul odor" in Egypt (Exodus 7:21). The message Christ produces both good odor and bad odor, both life and death.

The apostle Paul said, 1 *14But thanks be to God, who always leads us as captives in Christ's triumphal procession and uses us to spread the aroma of the knowledge of him everywhere. 15For we are to God the pleasing aroma of Christ among those who are being saved and those who are perishing.* **16To the one we are an aroma that brings death;** *to the other, an aroma that brings life (1 Corinthians 2:14-16, NIV).*

The false prophets then did the same act as Moses with their enchantments, and God is allowing the same deception in this age. There is also a false message concerning Jesus' blood that is being preached that creates death (self-condemnation) and a foul smell (more conscious of one's wrong doings, rather than being conscious of Jesus' righteousness imparted to us by His blood). These Jannes and Jambres types are preaching "condemnation" instead of Jesus' surpassing grace and justification by Jesus' grace.

Another practical application of blood being reproduced by the Jannes and Jambres is this: the "foul smell" of some people always being in a state of "dead work" (their conscience not purged by Jesus' blood to "serve the living God"[6]). Some are also

---

[6] Hebrews 9:14; Hebrews 6:1, etc.

more conscious of "their" past evil doings, rather than having a "good conscience"[7] of believing what Jesus' blood has accomplished for them through forgiveness.

Saying it yet another way, some preach "the blood of another" (righteousness by works) that speaks "weaker things" (sin consciousness). On the contrary, the true message of the "New Testament in [Jesus'] blood" "speaks 'stronger' things"[8] ("no remembrance of sins"[9]). Blood is related to covenant[10] (testament) as seen in the previous paragraphs.

In this age, breaking covenant is common. Blood is being abused relative to covenant with Jesus, covenant in marriages, trust, sexuality, murder, rape, and so on. However, abuse of blood brings "punishment." For Example, those who abuse the blood of Jesus will eventually be "punished" by God.

*Hebrews 10:29, NIV: How much more severely do you think a man deserves to be punished who has trampled the Son of God under foot, who has **treated as an unholy thing the blood of the covenant** that sanctified him, and who has insulted the Spirit of grace?*

If the Church abuses the blood of Jesus, there is punishment associated with that abuse. God does not like the abuse of blood in any form. God even demands the "accounting from every animal" that shed blood (Genesis 9:4-6). This is the truth. God judged Egypt with blood because they were shedding the blood of babies, and blood related to enslaving people. There are also many "so-called" religions and secret societies that require the shedding of blood for initiation into their beliefs.

---

[7] Hebrews 10:22
[8] Hebrews 12:24
[9] Hebrews 10:17; Hebrews 8:12
[10] Hebrews 13:20

This bloodshed ranges from branding to literal murdering of humanity. The druids sacrificed children annually, worshiping Satan, Baal, or Molech (Ezekiel 16:21, Leviticus 18:21, Isaiah 57:3-5, etc). Remember the four hundred and fifty "prophets of Baal"—1 King 18:25—when they encountered Elijah in 1 Kings 18:19-40. Listen to what they did when their limited power was being exposed by Elijah: *"So they shouted louder and slashed themselves with swords and spears, as was their custom, until their blood flowed"* (2 Kings 18:28; Philippians 3:2).

The many forms of witchcraft and divination use blood as an initiation—animals' and/or humans.' Diviners use the "liver" for divination (Ezekiel 21:21). This means an animal had to shed blood for them to get the liver. What is my point? God judged Egypt with blood because they were shedding blood in the land with all their abominable practices. There will come a time in the earth when God judges the earth again by turning water into literal blood!

*Revelation 16: 4-7, NIV: [4]The third angel poured out his bowl on the rivers and springs of water, **and they became blood**. [5]Then I heard the angel in charge of the waters say: "You are just in these judgments, O Holy One, you who are and who were; [6]for they have shed the blood of your holy people and your prophets, and you have given them blood to drink as they deserve." [7]And I heard the altar respond: "Yes, Lord God Almighty, true and just are your judgments."*

*Revelation 11:6, NIV: They [the two witnesses] have power to shut up the heavens so that it will not rain during the time they are prophesying; and they have power to **turn the waters into blood** and to strike the earth with every kind of plague as often as they want.*

In Genesis 9:5 God says that He requires an "accounting" for "lifeblood." It is so serious to God that if an animal kills a man that animal must give an account to God. *"And for your lifeblood I will surely demand an accounting. I will demand an accounting from every animal. And from each man, too, I will demand an accounting for the life of his fellow man" (Genesis 9:5).* People's bloodshed[11] is serious to God. Therefore, all who abuse blood are forming a covenant with the Devil; and they must give an account. The false prophets and all who shed blood in the world will be judged by blood, similarly to Egypt, if they do not turn from their evil practices and become a disciple of Jesus. Listen to the Revelation of Jesus Christ.

*Revelation 8:7, NIV: The first angel sounded his trumpet, and there came hail and **fire mixed with blood**, and it was hurled down upon the earth. A third of the earth was burned up, a third of the trees were burned up, and all the green grass was burned up.*

*Revelation 8:8-9, NIV: 8 The second angel sounded his trumpet, and something like a huge mountain, all ablaze, was thrown into the sea. A third of **the sea turned into blood**, 9 a third of the living creatures in the sea died, and a third of the ships were destroyed.*

*Revelation 16:3-7, NIV: 3The second angel poured out his bowl on the sea, and it turned into blood like that of a dead man, and every living thing in the sea died. 4The third angel poured out his bowl on **the rivers and springs of water, and they became blood.** 5Then I heard the angel in charge of the waters say: "You are just in these judgments, you who are and who were, the Holy One, because you have so judged; 6for they have shed the blood of your saints and prophets, and you have given them blood to drink as they deserve." 7And I heard the altar respond: "Yes, Lord God Almighty, true and just are your judgments."*

God judged Egypt with blood because of the innocent blood they shed when they killed the "boy" children of the Jews (Exodus 1:15-22). Through slavery, the Egyptians were also shedding the blood of God's Church of that day (Israel in the days of Moses

---

[11] Refer to my book, *The Lamb*, chapter 1, for further development on how to be freed from the guilt of bloodshed in its many forms.

were also called "Church" Acts 7:38). They were trying to get to the "male" seed—Moses, Aaron, Joshua, Caleb. The same is occurring and will occur in the religious harlot supported by the beast system!

*Revelation 17:6, NIV: I saw that the **woman [mystery Babylon]** was drunk with the **blood of God's holy people**, the blood of those who bore testimony to Jesus.*

*Revelation 18:24, NIV: In **her [mystery Babylon]** was found **the blood** of **prophets** and of **God's holy people, of all who have been slaughtered on the earth.**"*

The world shall be judged in the same manner for doing the same thing. The blood of the prophets and saints shall be accounted for. Even, the prophets killed in/by abortionist before they were born. Prophets do not become prophets over night. God placed them in their mother's womb as prophets (Jeremiah 1:5).

A sign that the seed of God is being birthed in this season is the escalation of abortion in the earth. The dragon is personally trying to kill the seed of God through humans (Revelation 12; Matthew 2:1-18; Exodus 1:15-22). Remember in the book of Revelation they were given blood to drink because they shed blood. Listen to the scripture. *"For they have shed the blood of your saints and prophets, and you have given them blood to drink as they deserve"* (Revelation 16:6).

I will now conclude with the frogs. There are spirits that look like frogs. The strange thing about this truth is that the dragon, the beast, and the false prophet have their own frog spirits. Yet we know that at least two of them do not look like a frog.

*Revelation 16:12-14, NIV: 12The sixth angel poured out his bowl on the great river Euphrates, and its water was dried up to prepare the way for the kings from the East. 13Then I saw **three evil spirits that looked*** *like frogs; they came out of the mouth of the dragon, out of the mouth of the beast and out of the mouth of the false prophet.*

As seen in the verses above, the "frogs" of Egypt can point to "the evil (lit.; unclean) spirits that looked like frogs." A note in passing; I could expound on the gods of Egypt that had animal heads with human bodies. God said that his plagues were to also judge the gods (plural) of Egypt (Exodus 12:12). Thus, the Egyptians must have had a god with a frog's head. I suggest you study them in contrast of the cherubs of God (Ezekiel 1). One symbolism of the frogs was the fact that Egypt had "unclean sprits" in their land. Frogs also points to false signs that deceive. Considering Revelation 16:13a, the frogs that Moses produced points to "evil or unclean spirits" that judged Egypt. The purpose of the frogs was to judge Egypt for all their uncleanness.

Principle: The very unclean thing a person uses, God will cause that uncleanness to multiply in judgment against the user.

This is what God did to Egypt. Egypt apparently worshipped frogs, therefore, God judged them by multiplying frogs (demons). In the book of Revelation 16:13, the dragon multiplied by reproducing a frog spirit. The beast did the same thing and so did the false prophets. These frogs represent demons. Hence, the people of the earth were also worshipping demons (Revelation 9:20-21). In addition, Psalms 105:30 states that God multiplies frogs in the chamber of the kings of Egypt. The same is true today, demonic activities are multiplying in the chambers of the leaders of the world for an eventuality of fighting against Jesus and His Church (Revelation 16:12-16 w/Revelation 19:19-21).

All those who indulge with demonic false prophets—psychics, the palm readers, necromancers, warlocks, sorcerers, Satan worshippers, wizards (male witches), witches, believers in the new age movement, false teachers in the Church, and so on will be judged by the same secret arts they use. God will cause the lives of the indulgers to be tormented miserable by the stench of uncleanness for using unclean spirits (Exodus 8:13). God will also allow "false signs" to deceive some of those who refuse the "love of the Truth."

Yet, the Lord, through His Church is also judging the false prophets. Jesus and His Church shall take the dragon by his tail and expose the prophets who teach lies. Why? He wants to deliver the oppressed. He wants to release some out of the "spirit of Egypt." God's expectation is that some will "love the Truth.'

It is never too late to stop unclean indulgencies with false prophets. You can be saved. The blood of Jesus is stronger than any blood that may have you bound by a false covenant. Do not believe the lie that you were born or destined to be a witch, warlock, necromancer, etc (Acts 19:18-19, NIV). The road to freedom may not be easy for a person—this "person" may be "you." However, our God is all-powerful. All things are possible with Him, including your deliverance from every evil covenant and an evil conscience.

*Matthew 19:26, NIV: Jesus looked at them and said, "With man this is impossible, but **with God all things are possible.**"*

He will protect you. Once you get saved in truth, our God will hide you in Christ Jesus. Colossians 3:1-4 says that after we believe in the Lord Jesus and seek those things that are above in heaven, we will be "hidden with Christ in God." Psalms 91: 4 say, "He will cover you with his feathers, and under his wings you will find refuge; his faithfulness will be your shield and rampart."

THE TALE

*Revelation 13:14-15, NIV: [14]Because of the signs he was given power to do on behalf of the first beast, he deceived the inhabitants of the earth. He ordered them to set up an image in honor of the beast who was wounded by the sword and yet lived. [15]He was given power to give breath to the image of the first beast, so that it could speak and cause all who refused to **worship the image to be killed.***

*Revelation 13:4, NIV: **Men worshiped the dragon** because he had given authority to the beast, and they also **worshiped the beast** and asked, "Who is like the beast? Who can make war against him?"*

*Romans 1:25, NIV: They exchanged the truth of God for **a lie (lit.; the lie)** and **worshiped and served** created things rather than the Creator-who is forever praised. Amen.*

The previous chapter of this book showed that the "tail" of the dragon (Satan) is the "prophets who teach lies." This tail also propagates "the tale." One of the most prominent "tales" of false prophets is "the lie" of creature worship. In the mind of most people when the word "lie" is mentioned, they probably think of "a fib" (Genesis 12:11-20). This is partially true. However, "the lie" is a little deeper than that, based on Biblical teaching.

The lie has to do with humans worshiping other humans, humans worshipping the beast and dragon [(both created beings/things); humans worshipping manmade objects, etc. (Romans 1:25; Revelation 13:4)]. The emphasis here is on "created things." Before I explain the lie in detail with reference to worship of the created things instead of worshipping the Creator, I will show how "the lie" is linked to the false prophets.

THE LIE AND ANTICHRISTS

The liar is "the man who denies that Jesus is the Christ. Such a man is the antichrist—he denies the father and the son" (1 John 2:22). The antichrist is the liar. 1 John 4:1-3 teaches that the "many false prophets" are "the spirit of antichrist." One can logically conclude that the false prophets are one of the faces of the antichrists. The antichrists are "the liars." 1 John 2:22 asks, "Who is the liar?" The same verse then gave the answer: "It is the man who denies [or contradicts] that Jesus is the Christ."

Therefore, the Devil, who is the father of lies, must have denied the God/Man Jesus in the beginning (Good study). It is from this point of view; I will expound to you how to recognize the lie. A purpose of my exposing this lie is to keep some from falsehood. I have taught this to a degree in *The False Prophet, Alias, Another Beast.* Therefore, for the most part, I will teach in this chapter that which was not included in the that volume.

SPEAKING FROM HIS OWN

*John 8:44, KJV: You are of your father the Devil, and the lusts of your father you will do. He was a murderer from the beginning, and abode not in the truth, because there is no truth in him. When he **speaks a lie**, he speaks **of** his own: for he is a liar, and the father of it.*

"The lie" is a profoundly serious topic, and it links to one of the deepest statements I think Jesus said. With that said, we will begin this study at John 8:44: "When he [the Devil] speaks a lie (lit., the lie), he speaks **of** (lit., out of) his own." Therefore, speaking "the lie" has to do with speaking "out of" one's "own" self. Our Lord Jesus is opposite the statement above. Listen to what I believe is one of the deepest statements Jesus said. *"**I can of mine own self do nothing**: as I hear, I judge and my judgment is just; because I seek not mine own will, but the will of the Father which hath sent me"* (John 5:30, KJV).

You may say "Brother Donald why is this statement so 'deep'?" Jesus said, "I can of mine own self do nothing." The word "of" means: "from" in the Greek. The verse should read, "I can **'from'** mine own self do nothing." **This means that Jesus did nothing that originated from himself.** Everything that Jesus did was because Jesus' heavenly Father told Him to do it; or because He saw His father do it (John 5:19). In other words, the statement is talking about absolute reliance on God's approval to do a task before the task is embarked upon. **Jesus did absolutely "nothing" on His own.**

Jesus' statement is deep because we would not sin if we stopped living "from" our own self. It is deep because; it means absolute death to self. It is deep because we are not living this truth absolutely. If we were not seeking our "own will," all the Father's will would be done in earth as it is being done in the heavens, now. Most of anything that has its origin "from" fallen mankind and fallen angels is "the lie."

Remember, the lie of the Devil is that he speaks "out of" his "own" self. Before Dr. Turnel Nelson of Trinidad and Tobago went to be with the Lord, he told us "God <u>cannot</u> lie,[12] and the devil <u>cannot</u> tell the truth." He also told us that "mankind is the only being that can tell both truth and lie." The Church, through grace, must live opposite the lie of the Devil. We, like Jesus, must strive to do nothing from our self. We must seek His will, "know the truth," and speak truth out of the Spirit of Truth. False prophets are the opposite and always speak from themselves.

Ezekiel 13:1-3, NIV: [1]The word of the LORD came to me: [2]"Son of man, prophecy against the prophets of Israel who are now prophesying. Say to those who prophesy out of their own imagination: 'Hear the word of the LORD! [3]This is what the Sovereign LORD says: **Woe to the foolish prophets who follow their own spirit** *and have seen nothing!*

---

[12] Hebrews 6:18; Titus 1:2

This is the difference between the Devil's prophets and God's holy prophets. The Devil's prophets do what the Devil does. They speak out of their "own" imagination. They follow their "own" spirits, which are unclean. Thus, they are liars. However, on the contrary, the Lord controls the spirits of the true prophets. He is the God of the spirits of the true prophets.

*Revelation 22:6, BLB: And he said to me, "These words are faithful and true. And the Lord, **the God of the spirits of the prophets,** sent His angel to show His servants the things that must come to pass in quickness."*

God's prophets are special to Him! They have submitted their spirits to the living God (Romans 1:9, 2 Timothy 4:22, Philemon 25). They do not "speak from their own selves." They are only "carried along" or "moved" by the Holy Spirit (2 Peter 1:21). Prophets whose spirits are controlled by the Lord do not have their own private interpretation.

IDIOTS

2 Peter 1:20-21, NIV: [20]Above all, you must understand that no prophecy of Scripture came about by the prophet's own interpretation. [21]For prophecy never had its origin in the will of man, but men spoke from God as they were carried along by the Holy Spirit.

The word "own" is the Greek word "idias." The word "idiot" is transliterated from this Greek word and is used in several places in the New Testament (Greek for: ignorant—Acts 4:13, KJV; 2 Peter 3:5; 3:8, KJV; and the Greek word for "rude" —2 Corinthians 11:6, KJV). In the culture of ancient Greek, it was customary for some to go to the market square and confer with at least two or three persons on topics. An idiot was an individual who would not confer with the group. He would go off to himself and have his own private interpretation or "ideas." Thus, false prophets are idiots with their own ideas. They only listen to the thoughts of their own hearts. There is no communion between their spirits and the God of the spirits of all mankind (Numbers 16:22, Jeremiah 23:21-22). The Holy Spirit says, *"How long will this continue in the hearts of these lying prophets, who prophesy the delusions of their own minds" (Jeremiah 23:26)?* False prophets, like Satan, speak from their own minds.

They do not gather with the Godhead—Father, Son and Holy Spirit—to receive words from God. They are not teachable. Instead, they seek counsel from their own fallen heart. They refuse the "counsel" of the Lord (Jeremiah 23:22). According to Peter, they are "idiots." "Okay Brother Peart I hear you, but **how do I know when prophets are idiots**—speaking from their own selves?"

CHOOSE GOD'S CHOICE!

*John 7:17-18, NIV: If anyone **chooses to do God's will,** he will find out whether my teaching comes from (Gk.; "ek"—out of) God or whether I speak on (Gk.; "Apo"—from) my own. [18]He who speaks on (Gk.; from) his own does so to gain honor for himself, but he who works for the honor of the one who sent him is a man of truth; there is nothing false about him.*

Jesus gave the answer as to how to know those who are speaking or teaching from their own heart and mind. *"If anyone chooses to do God's will, he will find out whether my teaching comes from God or whether I speak on my own."* Remember, idiots are like the Devil who was the first to speak from his own private (ideological) interpretation concerning himself (You may reference one of my other books for additional development, *"Son of Man Prophesy Against the False Prophet"*). Concerning the true believer, Jesus said, *"There is nothing false about him"* – the one who works for God's honor (John 7:18). If there is "nothing false" about the man who does God's will, there must be "something false" about those who speak and do things from themselves.

The answer the Lord gave may be subjective to you if you are not spiritual. That is, the way a person knows God's teaching is by choosing God's will[13]. It is not ascertained by physical appearance. Jesus said, "If anyone chooses to do God's will...." — the Greek structure of this phrase reads, "If anyone chooses His (God's) choice he will know." There is a difference between knowing and discerning. We may discern by mental separation or we may know by the Holy Spirit without human effort (Mark 2:8).

The key to knowing if a preacher, prophets, etc. are speaking from themselves is to choose God's choice for your life. This means accept that which God has chosen for your life and you will be able to know doctrine. Everyone — deep, deep, deep in their hearts knows what God's choice is for their lives. God's choices may include general directives or time specific directives. They may be explicit or implicit. Here is an example of a word the Lord spoke to me audibly internally.

GOD'S CHOICE — CALLED TO BE A SON

*Ephesians 1:5, NIV: He predestined us for **adoption to sonship (lit., son-placing)** through Jesus Christ, in accordance with his pleasure and will.*

---

[13] Here are some clear examples of the objective or "stated" **will of God** that should we should "choose:" Jesus has made us clean through the offering of His body (Hebrews 10:10), sanctification by abstaining from sexual immorality (1 Thessalonians 4:3), giving God thanks "in" everything (1 Thessalonians 5:18), "doing good," (1 Peter 2:15), water baptism (Luke 7:30), the work of harvesting people to serve the Father and/or Christ (John 4). God's subjective will can be ascertained through prayer (2 Corinthians 8:5), and/or the Volume of the Scriptures (Hebrews 10:7-10).

2.6.05: While on a fast (13 days), the Lord reminded me of a word He tried to speak to me around 1988, in North Carolina. At that time (1988) the voice said, **"I have not called you to be an apostle, [...], evangelist, pastor, teacher, but a [...]"** As God was speaking with me, I blocked out "prophet" at the beginning of God's conversation with me and I blocked out the rest of what he wanted to say to me at the end of His conversation. At the time I was afraid of what God would speak contrary to what I wanted to be—a prophet). Seventeen years later, yes, seventeen years later, on <u>February</u> 6, 2005, in Maryland while I was on my knees by the sofa praying, during 13 days of fasting, the Lord resumed His discourse again, exactly the way He attempted to speak to me the first time in 1988. He reminded me how He tried to speak to me in 1988 and how I had blocked out His words. The voice of the Lord continued exactly as He spoke in 1988, **"I have not called you to be a prophet, an apostle, an evangelist, a pastor or teacher, but a son."** I have chosen God choice for my life. I am a son, as He as said. God's will for us is to be His sons through Jesus Christ!

Galatians 4:3-7, BSB: [3]So also, when we were children, we were enslaved under the basic principles of the world. [4]But when the time had fully come, God sent His Son, born of a woman, born under the law, [5]to redeem those under the law, that we might receive our **adoption as sons**. *[6]And because you are sons, God sent the Spirit of His Son into our hearts, crying out, "Abba, Father!" [7]So you are no longer a slave,* **but a son;** *and* **since you are a son,** *you are also an heir through God.*

REEVALUATING OUR CHOICES

As we choose God's choices, the Church will be able to know the differences between the ones who are prophesying from their own heart rather than the heart of God. This kind of knowing is internal. You cannot concentrate on how a person looks and dresses. They may have the finest clothes, finest cars, and houses.

Or they may be a person who does not dress so well, poor, etc. Outward appearance cannot be the ultimate measure (1 Samuel 16:7). All the sincere ones must choose Jesus' choice to be able to understand doctrine whether the doctrine is of God. We—the Church—must reevaluate ourselves.

We must see if all the things we say, "God said" is true or not. A friend once told me that he decided to write down everything that would "appear" to be God speaking to him for a certain period. He did this for approximately eight months. After the eight months, he concluded that if God had told him to do all the things he wrote down, God would have been confused and crazy. He evaluated himself with the standard of Jesus!

His point was to show that we should not follow everything that comes into our "own" heart, without God's independent witness. The Church must not be so quick to say, "God said" and God did not say. False prophets, according to Ezekiel and Jeremiah, speak from their own hearts and not from the heart of God (Jeremiah 28:2). They claim to hear from God (Jeremiah 28:2), however, these false prophets heard lies (Jeremiah 28:15-17; 27:9-10; 23:9-18).

Now, as stated in the beginning of this chapter, I will show through the Word how "the lie" is linked to creature worship. In John 8:44 (KJV) Jesus said, "the devil…speaks a lie." Again, the Greek structure says, "the Devil speaks "the lie." What is "the lie?" One facet of "the lie" is speaking from one's own self. Another facet of "the lie" is creation worshipping creation."

THE LIE-CREATURE WORSHIP

Revelation 13:4, NIV: **Men worshiped the dragon** *because he had given authority to the beast, and* **they also worshiped the beast** *and asked, "Who is like the beast? Who can make war against him?"*

In the verse above men worshipped the dragon and the beast. This is most detestable to God. You may say, "Why is that?" The depth of the statement above is in the spirit. The statement in the verse above is synonymous with homosexuality/lesbianism—now do not close the book. I am not judging homosexuals and lesbians without understanding that God saves those who repent (1 Corinthians 6:9-11). In addition, Jesus also healed catamites (Matthew 4: 23). With that said, in the verse above, we see the created beings (men) worshiping other created beings (the dragon and the beast). What does this have to do with homosexuality? Homo is the Greek word for "same." Sexuality is defined as the gender of a species.

Therefore, "same sex" means homosexuality/lesbianism. "Worship" also means to kiss (Vines Dictionary, Strong's Concordance). It is a very intimate word. Therefore, creature worshipping creature is the same as men having copulation with men or women having sexual relations with women Romans 1:23 through Romans 1:27 made this clear. All created things are of the same gender in this sense: they are "created things." The Creator is in a class by Himself (Isaiah 44:8). He is The Creator. Therefore, created things worshiping created things are just like homosexual acts.

Creatures (mankind, angels, animals) were created to worship the Creator—God—not other creatures. And for those who do not believe there is the living God, they are lying. God shows Himself to every human (Romans 1:28). I remember as a young boy in Jamaica, West Indies, I was walking through the walkway a jot past the gate to the property. At that moment it appears that I was transfixed between heaven and earth; and I looked up and said, "Surely there must be a God." That was God revealing Himself to me at a young age. I was not brought up in Church; however, I realized there must be a Creator. His name is Jesus. God reveals Himself in every creature (Romans 10:18). However, mankind still insists on creature worship.

This creature worship is the lie the Devil fathered. The Devil fathered the concept of man and angels (created beings) worshiping him, his idols (images of created things); animals (created things), instead of God (the Creator), and so on. Satan spoke of his own self (John 8:44); he spoke of his own worship (Luke 4:6-8). He caused other created things—angels and men—to kiss Him instead of the Christ.

*Romans 1:25, NIV: They exchanged **the truth** of God for **a lie (lit; the lie) and worshiped and served created things** rather than the **Creator**—who is forever praised. Amen.*

Paul said that anyone who "exchanged the truth of God for the lie" is the same as one who worships and serves the "created things" rather than the "Creator." *"22Although they claimed to be wise, they became fools 23and exchanged the glory of the immortal God for images made to look like mortal man and birds and animals and reptiles"* (Romans 1:22-23).

The lie, according to Romans 1:25 quoted above, is when the created things (mankind/angels) worship other created things (each other), which range from excessive love of animals to worshipping human body parts more than the living God. In Revelation 13 the people worshipped the "dragon"—a "reptile" and the "beast"— a four footed animal which also points to man and his government systems that is anti-God and ruled by beast-spirits (See Daniel 7, Daniel 10). In Revelation 13, they worshipped the "image of the beast", which in the words of Romans 1:23, is "images made to look like … animals."

As you can see, Revelation 13 lines up with Romans 1:23 perfectly, it does not stop there. Paul said God then judged these creature worshippers to "imaged" in sexual life what they were doing with their idols. Creature was worshiping creature of the same species — the class of created things. Therefore, He allowed men to participate in anal[14] sex with men and women, and women having sexual relations with women "for the degrading of their bodies with one another" (Romans 1:24, 1:26, 1:27).

Therefore, in God's sight, whenever a person worships the creation — whales, dogs, birds, women/men body parts, athletes, idolized singers, preacher worship, self-worship, etc. — it is just like homosexual act. In fact, a lot of the people who do these things are usually homosexual, lesbian, bisexual, adulterers, fornicators, or sexually perverted.

Do a little research and you will see that the statement I just made is true! Creature worshiping creature is dirty in God's sight. Most animals are made to be eaten (Genesis 9:2-3; 1 Corinthians 6:13, 1 Timothy 4:4-5), not worshiped. This does not mean that we abuse animals. We are instructed to take care of our animals (Proverb 12:10, NIV). The question is though: "Can the homosexuals, lesbians and bisexuals receive deliverance?" Yes! Some will be saved.

*1 Corinthians 6:9-11, NIV: 9Do you not know that the wicked will not inherit the kingdom of God? Do not be deceived: Neither the sexually immoral nor idolaters nor adulterers nor **male prostitutes** nor **homosexual offenders** 10nor thieves nor the greedy nor drunkards nor slanderers nor swindlers will inherit the kingdom of God. 11And that is what some of you were. But you were washed, you were sanctified, you were justified in the name of the Lord Jesus Christ and by the Spirit of our God.*

Paul said, **"And that is what some of you were."** Therefore, those who "are homosexual offenders," the spiritual homosexuals who

---

14 Note: I will not take the time in this book to teach in detail about the reprobation of anal sex that is so popular in many countries, except to say, that the Scriptures teaches that fornication is also a source of anal sex.

worship the creatures—whales, cats, dogs, birds, self, and other humans instead of God can be saved. In the Name of the Lord Jesus Christ and by the Spirit of God they can be washed, sanctified, and justified. Yes! Yes! Yes! The same Christ that they deny is the same Christ that is extending His arm to forgive them.

In conclusion, do not be caught dead—literally—worshiping the creation. The penalty for that crime is eternal torment with fire and brimstone (Revelation 14:10-11). Revelation 17 said that those whose names <u>are not</u> written in the book of life will be the ones who worship the beast and his image—a creature. Are you worshipping beasts—four footed, or two footed men and women, world governments, etc.? Stop! It is the homosexual spirits of Satan, the beast and the false prophets that are the fathers of these acts. False prophets, the antichrists, will deny the Christ. They will cause worship of themselves and things other than God.

It is easy as a man or woman of God to allow people to worship him/her. But you must stop it. If you do not stop it (Revelation 22:8-9, Acts 10:25-26, Acts 14:9-15) homosexuality may be around the corner waiting for you. Let us get it clear, we should respect the man and woman of God (1 Thessalonians 5:12-13), but we should never worship fallen mankind in any form. There is a difference between respect and worship. False prophets, like Satan, want to steal God's kiss. Yet, true prophets will receive respect out of honor to their God (I Samuel 16:4). Why? They do not speak from their own heart or private interpretation. They do not do the lie. They do not deny the Father and the Son. I conclude:

1 John 2:22-23, NIV: ²² *Who is the liar? It is the man who denies that Jesus is the Christ. Such a man is the antichrist—he denies the Father and the Son.* ²³*No one who denies the Son has the Father; whoever acknowledges the Son has the Father also.*

MANY "TAIL"-BEARERS

*Revelation 16:13, NIV: Then I saw **three evil spirits** that looked like frogs; they came out of the mouth of **the dragon**, out of the mouth of **the beast** and out of the mouth of **the false prophet.***

*1 John 4:1, NIV: ¹Dear friends, **do not believe every spirit**, but **test the spirits** to see whether they are from God, **because many false prophets** have gone out into the world. ²This is how you can recognize the Spirit of God: Every spirit that acknowledges that Jesus Christ has come in the flesh is from God, ³ but every spirit that does not acknowledge Jesus is not from God. This is the spirit of the antichrist, which you have heard is coming and even now is already in the world.*

We learned previously in this book that Isaiah called prophets who teach lies as "the tail." These "tails" tell "tales;" and there are many "talebearers" in the earth today. These talebearers manifest themselves in "many" forms. For example, they are the "tail of the dragon;" and like the dragon himself, these false prophets bear "tales" (false prophecies).

These many "tails" are synonymous with the "many false prophets." This chapter will deal with the many forms through which the false prophet's spirit manifests itself. An important aspect to remember is that behind the "many false prophets" is "one spirit." The spirit of antichrist can reproduce or expand itself to cover "many false prophets."

In Revelation 16:13 cited above, we see that the three beasts could multiply themselves by releasing evil — lit.: "unclean" — spirits out of their mouths. The false prophet is included in the number above. If a false prophet prophesies over a person, he is releasing a frog spirit on that individual. In the land of Egypt, Moses multiplied the frogs in Egypt as a judgment. God (Moses in type — Exodus 7:1) is allowing a spirit like a frog to leave the false prophet's mouth to judge by deception (2 Thessalonians 2:9-11; Revelation 16:13). The reason why there is continuity among the false prophets is because there is one lying spirit among them.

ONE LYING SPIRIT IN THE MANY MOUTHS

2 Chronicles 18:22, NIV: "So now the LORD has put **a lying spirit** in the mouths of **these prophets** of yours. The LORD has decreed disaster for you."

In the verse above the scripture is plain. "A" (singular) lying spirit was in the "mouths" (plural) of the prophets (plural). In fact, this one lying spirit was in the "mouths" of "four hundred" (400) false prophets (2 Chronicles 18:5). Be careful about "the many false prophets" bearing witness with each other.

All the false prophets that prophesied to Jehoshaphat in 2 Chronicles 18 all said the same false words. "Go," they answered, "for God will give it into the king's hand" (2 Chronicles 18:5). They also said, "Attack Ramoth Gilead and be victorious," they said, "for the LORD will give it into the king's hand" (2 Chronicles 18:11).

They even used the name of the Lord. But we know from verse 22 that they prophesied by a lying spirit. The "tails" were telling "tales." However, the true prophet (Micaiah) was contrary to the many false prophets.

In fact, King Ahab hated this true prophet. This is indicative to all true prophets. True prophets are hated. Micaiah told the truth and was hated for it. His voice was apposite the "majority" prophets.

Principle: A true prophet is usually opposite the voice of the majority of those who have NOT heard from God.

2 Chronicles 18:17-22, NIV: *¹⁶Then Micaiah answered, "I saw all Israel scattered on the hills like sheep without a shepherd, and the LORD said, 'These people have no master. Let each one go home in peace."* *¹⁷The king of Israel said to Jehoshaphat, "Didn't I tell you that he never prophesies anything good about me, but only bad?"* *¹⁸Micaiah continued, "Therefore hear the word of the LORD: I saw the LORD sitting on his throne with all the host of heaven standing on his right and on his left.* *¹⁹And the LORD said,* **'Who will entice Ahab king** *of Israel into attacking Ramoth Gilead and going* **to his death there?'** *"One suggested this, and another that.* *²⁰Finally, a spirit came forward, stood before the LORD, and said, 'I will entice him.' "'By what means?' the LORD asked.* *²¹'I will go and be a lying spirit in the mouths of all his prophets,' he said. "'***You will succeed*** in enticing him,' said the LORD. 'Go and do it.'* *²²"So now* **the LORD has put a lying spirit** *in the mouths of these prophets of yours. The LORD has decreed disaster for you."*

It was a heavy word — death to the rebellious king — but Micaiah revealed the truth. In the same manner, this book is telling the truth concerning false prophets, false shepherds, false elders, wizards, witches, etc. The false prophets were prophesying **"success"** in a war that God obviously did not sanction for Ahab's benefit (2 Chronicles 18:12-19). There is "death" in this apparent "success." In verse 19 Micaiah declared, "And the LORD said, who will entice Ahab…. to his death there."

Principle: When <u>false</u> prophets prophesy success, there may be "death" in it.

"I see a house," they say but there might be death (overwhelming debt) in that house if it is attained out of season. I see you with a "new" husband. That "new" husband may not be a taken "husband" man. These statements may seem different; however, they are true. **I would like to say at this point, false prophets do not negate the work and words of the true prophets of God**

(Ephesians 4:11; Acts 11:27-30). Prophets from God also prophesy encouraging things. *"Judas and Silas, who themselves were prophets, said much to encourage and strengthen the brothers"* (Acts 15:32).

We have learned so far that "one" lying spirit can multiply among those who are false. This is the same thing that the Apostle John said. He taught that "the spirit of antichrist" exists among the "many false prophets."

They all have one "tale," "worldly success" without a consecrated lifestyle. They teach that if you acquire "capital" it is because you are godly, contrary to the Scripture (1 Timothy 5:5-10). Some emphasize, for example that success is measured by erecting a glorious natural building <u>in lieu</u> of building the holy spiritual house (God's people). Do you know that God calls a natural building "worldly?"

The "viewpoint" of the false prophets is to have success through the world's standards', not God's. Ahab and his wife Jezebel were full of witchcraft, covetousness, and murder. Yet, they wanted a word of "success" from God in their war affairs.

The viewpoint of the "worldly church" is to use or do witchcraft, sorcery, magic, and the like for their benefit, and then some want to ask God for "success" in troubling situation like Ahab did. The Church of Jesus Christ must understand that the spirit of antichrist speaks from the "viewpoint of the world."

MANY FALSE PROPHET'S WORLDLY VIEWPOINT

*1 John 4:1, NIV: Dear friends, do not believe every spirit, but test the spirits to see whether they are from God, because **many false prophets have gone out into the world.***

1 John 4:3, NIV: but every spirit that does not acknowledge Jesus is not from God. This is the spirit of the antichrist, which you have heard is *coming and even now is already **in the world.***

*1 John 4:5, NIV: They are from the world and therefore **speak from the viewpoint of the world**, and the world listens to them.*

The spirit (singular) of antichrist is the one among the "many false prophets," and they have a worldly point-of-view. What is the purpose of knowing this? Do not be carried away with every wind of the worldly doctrine by false prophets who condone the worldly attitudes of the lust of the flesh, lust of the eyes and the pride of life (1 John 2:15-16; 1 Timothy 6:3-10, NIV). The voice of the majority saying the same thing does not mean it is from God.

All of the false prophets of 2 Chronicles 18 were all bearing witness to each other. They all were saying "success." The reason is they all spoke from the one evil spirit. Today, the one spirit of antichrist is among the "many false prophets." In 2 Chronicles their words were <u>anti-God's</u> point-of-view. In the New Testament they are called <u>antichrists.</u> Their point-of-view is worldly, full of lust. All the false prophets were saying the same words which were contrary to God until Micaiah showed up with the real word from God.

Micaiah means "the one who is like God." In this Dark Age, the "Micaiah" will be contrary to those who depend on the deceptive witness of each other to please the "kings"—lustful prominent people in the Church and in the world. One of the false prophets' names is "Zedekiah son of Kenaanah." Zedekiah means right of Jah, or righteousness of Jah. Kenaanah is defined as humble, humiliated.

This means that among the false prophets there is a witness of false—outward humility. They also believe they have the "right" of God to say, "The Lord is saying thus and thus." But the truth is: there is an evil spirit of antichrist in their mouth and heart. In their private lives, they are "worldly"—full of the lust of the flesh, the lust of the eyes and the pride of life (1 John 2:16, KJV). Remember, when there are the "many" witnesses, it does not necessarily mean God is in it. There may be a "tail" wagging close by?

"Micaiah" in 2 Chronicles 18:17-22 typifies Jesus as the one "right" Prophet against all those who were liars on the Sanhedrin counsel that unjustly sentenced Jesus to be crucified. I am going to tell you a principle I learned from Dr. Kelley Varner concerning this age with respect to the four hundred (400) false prophets in 2 Chronicles 18 who I called the "leftovers" from the 850 false prophets, per 1 Kings 18:40. These may have been the prophets of Baal that Elijah challenged.

In this age for every 400-850 prophets there is only one (1), or two (2) "who is like God" (Micaiah or Elijah). Percentage wise, this is 0.12%-0.25%. Note: NOT twelve to twenty-five percent but point twelve percent (0.12%) to point twenty five percent (0.25%), meaning not even 1% of theses prophets were from God. Elijah was one among eight hundred and fifty. Micaiah was one among four hundred. In other words, out of every 451 to 851 prophets who say they are speaking from God only one (1), or two (2) may be true. The other 400 to 850 are probably not from God. In addition, true prophets must brace themselves to be slapped around for a little while by false prophets. The abusers among the many false prophets will "slap" the faces of some of the true prophets who expose them (Matthew 26:67; 2 Chronicles 18:23). It does not stop there though.

Those who are walking in the spirit of Elijah will slay the false prophets of this age with the words of God (1 Kings 18:40 with Revelation 11:5). As stated above, there is a spirit of antichrist that is prophesying worldly "success" without living a joined life with Jesus. 1 John 4: 5-6 and 1 John 2:16 teaches that the false prophets through the spirit of antichrist *"speak from the viewpoint of the world*

... This is how we recognize the Spirit of truth and the spirit of falsehood."

1 John 2:15-16, NIV: [15]*Do not love the world or anything in the world. If anyone loves the world, the love of the Father is not in him.*[16]*For everything in the world — the cravings of sinful man, the lust of his eyes and the boasting of what he has and does — comes not from the Father but from the world.*

Be watchful in this age. There are many false children who claim they are children of Jesus, but they are children of the lustful world. They use secret arts of hell (Isaiah 57:3; 57:9, KJV) and pretend to be of Jesus. Have you noticed that some palm readers houses' have crosses on them? Some even use the name of Jesus as they use their witchcraft and sorcery (compare Matthews 7:22). "The love of the father is not in them." They are "tail-bearers!"

They have stealthily crept into the lives of people — saved and unsaved — and claim to be of God. The fact of the matter is they are magicians. In today's terms they are called palm readers, witches, warlocks, sorcerers, psychics, etc. One of the many forms that false prophets will be displayed as is "Bar-Jesus."

FALSE PROPHETS POSING AS BAR JESUS

Acts 13:6, NIV: They traveled through the whole island until they came to Paphos. There they met a Jewish sorcerer and false prophet named Bar-Jesus ...

In Acts 13:1-5, Barnabas, and Saul (called Paul) were dispatched by the Holy Spirit for apostolic work. The first thing they encountered on their trip was a false prophet. And the interesting thing about this encounter is that the false prophet appeared to have the name of Jesus — "Bar-Jesus."

Principle: Typically, the first oppositions newly sent apostles and prophets will encounter are sorcerers.

Some may come and sit in a church and try to create disruption in the spirit which spills over in the natural. If the man/women of God do not deal with that/those witchcraft/witches right of way, he/she may have trouble in the area of being hindered. Let us see how Paul dealt with it. I will begin with the phrase "Bar-Jesus."

"Bar-Jesus" means "son of Jesus." This "sorcerer" was also a "Jew." This same so-called "son of Jesus," this same "Jew" is also called a "false prophet." This is easy to follow so far, right? There are principles in this event that may be applied to this age. First, I will explain the sorcerer being called "son of Jesus." Our Lord Jesus said, "For many will come in my name" (Matthew 24:5).

This means that "many" false ones will come using the "name" of Jesus. False prophets of the world will say they are of Jesus. How do they "say" this? A good example of this is they will use the cross as a sign (bait) on their palm reading houses. They may use the name of Jesus in pronouncing their spells. Some may even claim that they (individually) are the second coming of Jesus, himself. It goes further.

 Some of the false ones who claim to be of Jesus are false-pastors, false-teachers, false- evangelist, false-prophets, and false-apostles. I met a lady years ago that was a "pastor." I later found out that she read palms and performed divination. This is just the tip. There are so-called pastors who seek words from mediums like King Saul did (1 Samuel 28). There are some so-called preachers who get their words from mediums and they preach these "tales" in their pulpits on Sundays. The result of their folly will be death like Saul. How do you recognize these false prophets? We will see in a moment; and here is a hint with a play (pun) on words, they are "tail-bearers."

The next thing is that the false prophet is called a "Jew." This goes back to what Jesus said about false prophets coming in sheep's clothing. There are false prophets who claim to be Jews (Christians). They claim to be circumcised inwardly.

Romans 2:28-29, KJV: *²⁸For he is not a Jew, which is one outwardly; neither is that circumcision, which is outward in the flesh: ²⁹But he is a Jew, which is one inwardly; and circumcision is that of the heart, in the spirit, and not in the letter; whose praise is not of men, but of God.*

The fact of the matter is false prophets' acknowledgement of being a believer is outward. That is, they pretend to be saved — circumcised inwardly (Romans 2:29 with Colossians 2:11) — but their heart is filled with the "deceit and trickery" (Acts 8:10-22). The purpose of the spirit of the false prophet's trickery and deceit is to turn people from faith in Jesus. According to the Scriptures, false ones are also known for "perverting the 'immediate' ways of the Lord" (Acts 13:10c). The false prophet that Barnabas and Saul encountered was guilty of both (attempting to delay God's immediate ways and attempting turn a man from the faith).

Acts 13:6-8, NIV: *⁶They traveled through the whole island until they came to Paphos. There they met **a Jewish sorcerer and false prophet** named Bar-Jesus, ⁷who was an attendant of the proconsul, Sergius Paulus. The proconsul, an intelligent man, sent for Barnabas and Saul because he wanted to hear the word of God. ⁸But Elymas the sorcerer (for that is what his name means) **opposed** them and tried to turn the proconsul from the faith.*

The word warlock, a male witch, means "to break faith." The reason why faith is so hard to attain in some Churches is because warlocks are sitting in Church, including the pulpit, opposing everything that is of faith. The spirit of the false prophet like a frog is leaping about in some circles. This is the attitude that Barnabas and Saul encountered. The sorcerer **"opposed** them and tried to turn the proconsul from the faith." If there is a temptation to turn from the faith to call the psychic hotline, to see palm readers, to do necromancy, and so on, then an antichrist spirit may be present.

That froglike spirit is trying to break your faith in Jesus. The sign of this spirit is: no faith, no prayer life, no study life, no fasting life and so on. There is a judgment for these false prophets who turn people from the faith of Jesus Christ. God is raising apostles and prophets who will judge the false ones with swiftness and severity. This is the age when God is raising up Judges—prophetic apostles and apostolic prophets—to judge as Paul judged.

Acts 13:9-12, NIV: *⁹Then Saul, who was also called* **Paul, filled with the Holy Spirit,** *looked straight at Elymas and said,* *¹⁰"You are a child of the devil and an enemy of everything that is right! You are full of all kinds of deceit and trickery. Will you never stop perverting the right (or immediate) ways of the Lord?* *¹¹Now* **the hand of the Lord is against you. You are going to be blind,** *and for a time you will be unable to see the light of the sun." Immediately mist and darkness came over him, and he groped about, seeking someone to lead him by the hand.* *¹²When the proconsul saw what had happened, he believed, for he was amazed at the teaching about the Lord.*

Did you hear that? The Holy Spirit filled Saul now called Paul. Paul was not terrified—Jeremiah 1:17—he "looked straight at Elymas and said, *"The hand of the Lord is against you. You are going to be blind...."* God has established prophets and apostles who will look at false prophets straight in their eyes and judge the evil. How will this judgment manifest?

"The hand of the Lord" will be "against" them and the Lord will do His judgment "immediately." The result of the judgment is that people will "believe." They will fear the Lord and get "right" really quick. "When the proconsul saw what had happened, he believed, for he was amazed at the teaching about the Lord" (Acts 13:12). In conclusion of this chapter, I will discuss the controversial matter of money. One of the marks of false prophets is the merchandising of the saints. I will explain this with balance.

FALSE TEACHERS MARKETING GREED

Revelation 13:16-17, NIV: ^{16}*He also forced everyone, small and great, rich, and poor, free and slave, to receive a mark on his right hand or on his forehead,* ^{17}*so that no one could* **buy or sell** *unless he had the mark, which is the name of the beast or the number of his name.*

2 Peter 2:1-3, NIV: ^{1}*But there were also false prophets among the people, just as there will be false teachers among you. They will secretly introduce destructive heresies, even denying the sovereign Lord who bought them — bringing swift destruction on themselves.* ^{2}*Many will follow their shameful ways and will bring the way of truth into disrepute.* ^{3}*In their greed these teachers* **will exploit you** *with stories they have made up. Their condemnation has long been hanging over them, and their destruction has not been sleeping.*

False prophets will "exploit" the saints. "Exploit" in the Greek is "emporeuomai" — this is where we get our English word emporium. "Emporeuomai" translates in the King James as "buy and sell" and "merchandise." The New International Version also translates it as "carry on business." In Revelation 13:17 we learn that buying and selling involves the "mark" of the beast. "Mark" is defined as "character" from the Greek "charagma."

Therefore, if prophets travel to Churches and use Jesus' Churches as a "money making business," it is because they have the character (mark) of the beast in their minds or foreheads (Revelation 13:16). The Church has become a marketplace ("a den of thieves") for false prophets. They will not come to your Church unless there is a "price." They have reduced the Church to a "business." The "Dove", Holy Spirit's anointing[15], now has a price in the Church (John 2:16 with Luke 3:22).

Micah 3:9-11, NIV: [9]*Hear this, you leaders of the house of Jacob, you rulers of the house of Israel, who despise justice and distort all that is right;* [10]*who build Zion with bloodshed, and Jerusalem with wickedness.* [11] **Her leaders judge for a bribe, her priests teach for a price,** *and her* **prophets tell fortunes for money.** *Yet they lean upon the LORD and say,* **"Is not the LORD among us?** *No disaster will come upon us."*

God is troubled over what is going on in "Zion" — the Church (Hebrews 12:22). Listen: "Her leaders judge for a bribe, her priests teach for a price, and her prophets tell fortunes for money." It does not stop there. The have the impudence to say, "Isn't this an anointed service." In the words of Micah, "they lean upon the LORD and say, "Is not the LORD among us?"

The Lord is not among them. It is not an anointed service. According to Revelation 13 they have the mark of the beast, because they are merchandising God's people. I have been in Churches where if you do not give a certain amount to the preacher, they make you feel small.

I have been in Church services where the length of prophesies depended on how much a person gave. The $1000 line got long prophesies. The $25 line received short prophesies. I have seen a so-called preacher stop the meeting to "sell" books and said the meeting would not go on until someone buys his book. He then made "war" on those who did not have the money to buy his book by calling them "poor." Do you know that the false

---

[15] Note: I am aware that "oil" can be sold to pay debts and feed one's family (2 Kings 4:1-7). However, "merchandising" God's anointing and His gospel for the express purpose of accumulating wealth fills one with "violence" and "sin" (Ezekiel 28:16; 1 Timothy 6:3-10).

prophets in Micah's days did the same thing? They made "war" on those who did not "feed" them.

Micah 3:5, NIV: This is what the LORD says: As for the prophets who lead my people astray, if one feeds them, they proclaim 'peace'; if he does not, they prepare to wage war against him.

This describes the false prophets of today. If you do not "feed" them with the amount of money they ask for, prepare for war. They will tear you down. They may say you will not have "peace," and try to use Malachi 3 to curse you. Cursing God's people is false doctrine. Did you know that Jesus Christ "redeemed us from the curse of the law" (Galatians 3:13)? There is a change of the priesthood from "law" — which involves curses — to "life" — which involves "blessings." "For when there is a change of the priesthood, there must also be a change of the law" (Hebrews 7:12). The law of cursing has been changed to the law of the Spirit of life which blesses (Romans 8:1-2, Hebrews 7:16).

Melchizedek "blessed" Abraham before Abraham "tithed" to him (Genesis 14: 18-20). The priesthood of Jesus should bless the people with life and the people will tithe. However, in Micah 3:10, the false prophets used "wickedness" to "build" Zion. God is going to expose this wicked building. He shall expose everything down to the foundation.

In Ezekiel 13, God spoke against the false prophets. He said that they built a "flimsy wall" with their false prophesies. The judgment was to tear down what was built upon wickedness. *"I will tear down the wall you have covered with whitewash and will level it to the ground so that its foundation will be laid bare. When it falls, you will be destroyed in it; and you will know that I am the LORD"* (Ezekiel 13:14).

God is going to expose the "foundation" of the false prophets.

They call themselves servants of Jesus. But they are not. Jesus is the true foundation (2 Corinthians 3:11). Therefore, when God said the "foundation will be laid bare," He means that He will expose the heart of these false prophets that all may see that Jesus is not in their lives. They have built Zion on the "evil" of the love of money. Their foundation is the love for money, not Jesus. It is more excellent to preach the Word of God for free. There is a reward in preaching the gospel without preset cost.

1 Corinthians 9:18, NIV: What then is my reward? Just this: that in preaching the gospel I may offer it free of charge, and so not make use of my rights in preaching it.

The reward of preaching the gospel is to offer it freely. It should give us pleasure to teach "free of charge." Jesus said, "freely you have received, freely give." We do not have to always "make use" of our "rights in preaching" the gospel. Now the balance to this is that the true believer should give to true men of God. It is their duty. They owe it to us. However, the man of God must not abuse this "right" by merchandising the people of God.

*Romans 15:25-27, NIV: 25 Now, however, I am on my way to Jerusalem in the service of the saints there. 26For Macedonia and Achaia were pleased to make a contribution for the poor among the saints in Jerusalem. 27They were pleased to do it, and indeed they owe it to them. For if the Gentiles have shared in the Jews' **spiritual blessings, they owe** it to the Jews to share with them their material blessings.*

The principle in the Scripture above is that if some partake of a spiritual blessing, they "owe it" to give "material blessings." Therefore, when the men of God teach the Church "spiritual" words, then the recipient should give their "material blessings." The King James Version translates it as "their duty" (Romans 15:27) to do this service.

*1 Corinthians 9:11, NJV: If we have sown **spiritual seed** among you, is* *it too much if we reap **a material harvest** from you?*

The Church must keep the verse above in mind for those who are of the Truth. The true men of God must also eat (1 Corinthians 9:4; 7; 10). According to the Scriptures, genuine men of God should not go to war on behalf of the Saints for free (1 Corinthians 9:7).

True prophets of God should also reap financial blessing from the Saints without the Church grumbling. But there is a qualification. The prophets of God must "sow spiritual seed" which according to Peter is the Word of God (1 Peter 1:23-25). If you are sowing carnality, then you should not get paid. In other words, if ministers are lazy and do not pray, study, or fast to receive a word from God they should not get paid.

1 Timothy 5:18, NIV: For the Scripture says, "Do not muzzle the ox while it is treading out the grain," and "The worker deserves his wages."

The "meat" in God's house is for the "ox" that "treads out the grain" who is worthy of double pay. Part of the tithe for the "storehouse" is to provide "food" for the ox (genuine men and women of God) (Malachi 3 w/1 Corinthians 9:1-10 and 1 Timothy 5:18). However, the very ones who are lazy and do not seek God, they pressure the Church to support their lazy attitude.

They do not tread out the Word. They do more stealing of messages from other men of God, rather than working to get their own spiritual words from the Father. Thus, they have to do marketing in order to pull money from the malnutrition people they are merchandising.

We must not allow the Church of the living God to become a marketplace, where leaders are using sales tactics and sale pressures to merchandise the Church of the living God. There are ways to offer the oil without pressuring the Saints. The true leader must exercise self-control and not put a price on the gospel and does not beg. Paul made a statement concerning money and self-control. Men of God quote it, but they do not understand it. If you do not believe me read the text again and see the logical link.

1 Corinthians 9:27, NIV: No, I beat my body and make it my slave so that after I have preached to others, I myself will not be disqualified for the prize.

In conclusion of this chapter, Paul made the statement above with respect to preaching the gospel without charge (see 1 Corinthians 9:1-21). There are many false prophets in the land. They are "disqualified for the prize." They have not disciplined their bodies not to always ask for money. Yes! It is a lack of discipline in false prophets' body that causes false prophets to merchandise the people of God.

It takes self-discipline not to ask for money and trust in God for supplies as He moves on the heart of His Saints to give. The false prophets who travel for the sake of money and those not disciplined enough to refrain from pressuring the Saints for money will be "disqualified." God will expose their foundation, and He will use genuine prophets to expose the false ones.

THE PROPHET'S INTERPRETATION

*Revelation 5:1-9, NIV: ¹Then I saw in the right hand of him who sat on the throne a scroll with writing on both sides and sealed with seven seals. ²And I saw a mighty angel proclaiming in a loud voice, **"Who is worthy to break the seals and open the scroll?"** ³But no one in heaven or on earth or under the earth could open the scroll or even look inside it. ⁴I wept and wept because no one was found who was worthy to open the scroll or look inside. ⁵ Then one of the elders said to me, "Do not weep! See, **the Lion of the tribe of Judah**, the Root of David, has triumphed. **He is able to open the scroll** and its seven seals." ⁶Then I saw **a Lamb** ... ⁷He went and took the scroll from the right hand of him who sat on the throne. ⁸And when he had taken it, the four living creatures and the twenty-four elders fell down before the Lamb. Each one had a harp ... ⁹And they sang a new song, saying: "**You are worthy to take the scroll and to open its seals ....***

Jesus is "the Prophet" (Matthew 21:10-13). If something is sealed from our understanding, it will take the true Prophet to open, or interpret the sayings of the living God. This true Prophet is Jesus, who is also the God of the spirits of His prophets. We have heard about the false prophets in this book; however, that does not negate the fact that there are indeed true prophets and apostles that exist today. Most in the Church are quick to say there are indeed false prophets.

Yet, some in the Church are not "quick" or willing to acknowledge that there are true prophets who understand the mystery of God (Revelation 10:7; Ephesians 3:1-6, etc.). The apostles' and prophets' interpretations are necessary. In fact, in this age, the mystery of His will for this generation will only be known through the apostles and prophets (Ephesians 3). However, the prophets of Jesus must receive their interpretation from "The Prophet" — Jesus. In Revelation 5:1-9 cited above, John, a prophetic apostle, was not worthy to open a book in God's hand, neither was he worthy to look in the book. The Lamb of God, the Prophet Jesus, was/is the only One worthy to "open the scroll" for John and the rest of the Churches to see and understand what is prewritten to happen. It takes the Prophet (Jesus) to give understanding of His words to His prophets. True apostles and prophets do exist today! Every prophet is not illegitimate, and apostles are not extinct.

APOSTLES AND PROPHETS UNTIL...

Ephesians 4:11-13, NIV: [11]It was he who gave some to be apostles, some to be prophets, some to be evangelists, and some to be pastors and teachers, [12] to prepare God's people for works of service, so that the body of Christ may be built up [14] until we all reach unity in the faith….

One of the reasons why "most" apostles and prophets are labeled as false today is because a lot of "pastors" do not believe in the apostle's and prophet's authority (Matthew 21:23-24). They (some pastors) are teaching lies when they say true prophets do not exists today. They go as far as forbidding the prophetic (Jeremiah 11:21; Amos 2:12; Amos 7:13-17; 1 Thessalonians 5:20). If pastors exist today, so do prophets and apostles. The same God who gave pastors is the One who gave apostles and prophets. Allow me to explain.

Ephesians 4:11, NIV: It was he who gave some to be apostles, some to be prophets, some to be evangelists, and some to be pastors and teachers.

*Ephesians 4:13, NIV: **Until** we all reach unity in the faith and in the knowledge of the Son of God and become mature, attaining to the whole measure of the fullness of Christ.*

"It was He [Jesus] who gave some to be apostles, some to be prophets… and some to be pastors and teachers." The Greek text for the first part of the phrase reads: "Kaí (And) autos (He) édooken (gave) toús (the) **mén (in fact)** apostólous (apostles)…"

The phrase above translated to English reads "And he gave **'in fact'** (**mén**) the apostles."

"Mén" according to Strong's Concordance is defined as: "a primary particle; properly, indicative of affirmation or concession (in fact); usually followed by a contrasted clause with NT: 1161 (this one, the former, etc)." Therefore, apostles' and prophets' existence are an "affirmation" of "fact." In fact, He gave them "until." "Until we all reach unity in the faith… of the Son of God!" "Until we all reach the unity … in the knowledge of the Son of God! Have "all" the Churches reached "unity in the faith and in the knowledge of the Son of God?" That is, have the saints attained to the same faith as the Son of God? Have the saints attained to the same knowledge as the Son of God? Obviously, the answer is no!

Pastors are needed to help the church "reach 'oneness' with Jesus' faith and knowledge, since Jesus is the standard of measure. Teachers are needed to help the church "reach oneness'." Evangelists are needed to help the church "reach 'oneness'." Prophets—yes prophets—are needed to help the church "reach 'oneness'." And last, but not least, Apostles are needed to help the church "reach 'oneness'." These five (5) gifts, not just three (3), all five (5) are given "until." "Until" is a time word. They are given until "all" the Church <u>attains</u> "to the whole measure of the fullness of Christ."

I repeat, if pastors, teachers, and evangelists exist today, then according to the logic of Ephesians 4:11-13, apostles and prophets exist today, "in fact." We are created with five fingers. If one is missing, it becomes difficult to use the hand properly. This is the same with the five-fold gifts. The Church has received the false prophets and rejected the true prophets. The reason why there are so many false ones in the Church is because the true prophets and apostles are not allowed to function properly. A Church will not mature properly unless she allows all five gifts to minister to the body. False prophets will not be eradicated without the function of true prophets (Jeremiah 28:16-<u>17</u>).

A car is made up of many components. If you remove the tires the car will not be able to go forward without the wheel. This is the same principle with apostles and prophets. Because they are missing from the body, the body will not go forward to maturity. If a part is missing, there will be deformity. If the apostles and prophets are missing, the body will be deficient. In fact, I am not so sure that people who have a deformed hand — one finger, which can symbolize a lone pastor — can draw near to offer food to his God. Note: I am referring to a spiritual principle, not people who are maimed physically.

*Leviticus 21:16-18, NIV: 16The LORD said to Moses, 17"Say to Aaron: 'For the generations to come none of your descendants who **has a defect may come near to offer the food of his God.** 18 No man who has any defect may come near: no man who is blind or lame, disfigured or deformed…"*

This is plain enough. God is always interested in a "whole" man. Paul said, "May God himself, the God of peace, sanctify you through and through. May your **whole** spirit, soul and body be kept blameless at the coming of our Lord Jesus Christ" (1 Thessalonians 5:23, NIV). This is that "perfect man" that the apostles and prophets will aid in perfecting — the Church — through the Spirit of Jesus Christ. Every part of the body is important. We need every part.

1 Corinthians 12:21, NIV: "The eye cannot say to the hand, "I don't need you!" And the head cannot say to the feet, "I don't need you!"

1 Corinthians 12:27-28, NIV: 27Now you are the body of Christ, and each one of you is a part of it. 28And in the church God has appointed first of all apostles, second prophets, third teachers, then workers of miracles, also those having gifts of healing, those able to help others, those with gifts of administration, and those speaking in different kinds of tongues.

The parts of the "body" are "apostles, second prophets, third teachers, then workers of miracles, also those having gifts of healing, those able to help others, those with gifts of administration, and those speaking in different kinds of tongues," and so on. All the pastors who decide to cut out the apostles and prophets; let them also cut themselves out. Let them say, "I will not recognize pastors anymore in the Church." Let us go a little further, let a Church say they do not need their pastor anymore.

That pastor would be discouraged; and the Church would go about without pastoral care. The same is true for apostles and prophets. The Church will lack apostolic knowledge and the prophetic scope. For example, the Church will lack sight and timing without the prophets and apostles, because prophets "see" and apostles "know."

It is not right for pastors to reject a part—apostles and prophets— of themselves. What if you decide to cut your thumb off? Will you be able to grasp an object properly? The answer is no! The same is true for the apostles and prophets. Most of the Church of today cannot "grasp" certain truths because their pastors, their evangelists and their teachers have rejected the prophetic and apostolic gifts. Do not be like the carnal Corinthians and say, "I don't need you!" The Lord is saying, "We need each other."

If you reject prophets today, you reject Jesus—Deuteronomy 18:15, John 4:19; 4:44; 6:14, 7:40, 9:17—because Jesus is "The Prophet." Matthew 21:11 says, the crowds answered, "This is **Jesus, the prophet** from Nazareth in Galilee." Sometimes it is only the crowds of people who are following Jesus who acknowledge true prophets. The leaders are too insecure and jealous to acknowledge apostles and prophets (Matthew 27:18; Acts 13:45).

If you reject apostles then you reject Jesus because, He is "the Apostle." *"Therefore, holy brothers, who share in the heavenly calling, fix your thoughts on **Jesus, the apostle** and high priest whom we confess" (Hebrews 3:1).* This same Apostle and Prophet gave apostles and prophets. In fact, He divided Himself into "many parts" (1 Corinthians 12:12).

He is The Apostle — He gave some to be apostles. He is The Prophet — He gave some to be prophets. He is The Evangelists — He gave some to be evangelists. He is The Good Shepherd — He gave some to be pastors. Finally, He is the Rabbi — He gave some to be teachers. Let the church embrace the rest of her "many parts" — apostolic and prophetic ministries. The apostles and prophets will cause the Church and the unsaved to understand the mysteries of God.

THE UNINTERPRETABLE

Genesis 41:1, NIV: When two full years had passed, Pharaoh had a dream: He was standing by the Nile …

Genesis 41:15, NIV: Pharaoh said to Joseph, "I had a dream, and no one can interpret it. But I have heard it said of you that when you hear a dream you can interpret it."

*Genesis 41:16, NIV: "I cannot do it," Joseph replied to Pharaoh, **"but God will give Pharaoh the answer he desires."***

Pharaoh had a dream "when two full years had passed" (Genesis 41:1). The Hebrew reads, "And it was at the end of two years of days that Pharaoh was dreaming." This is Hebrew rendering is significant prophetically. The "year-day" principle is seen in this verse.

The Church is "two years of days" from Jesus. The Apostle Peter in 2 Peter 3:8 said, *"But do not forget this one thing, dear friends: With the Lord **a day is like a thousand years**, and **a thousand years are like a day**."* A thousand years "with Lord is like one day; and one day is like a thousand years."

With respect to the Jesus, Pharaoh year-day dream points to the end of the two thousand years of days starting from Jesus' death, burial, and resurrection until approximately 2033, plus. Do you agree that 2000 AD is approximately two thousand years from Jesus' death burial and resurrection?

Therefore, according to Peter's 1,000 year equaling one day, we are approximately two days (2000+) from Jesus— "the last Adam" (1 Corinthians 15:45)—and close to the end of 6 days— 6000 years from "the first Adam" (1 Corinthians 12:12). Thus, a prophetic may be gained from the "timing" of the dream God gave Pharaoh. At the end of two years of days (2000+ years) from Jesus, God is causing the Pharaohs—all who claim to be leaders to dream, those ranging from drug dealers to presidents. Another way of saying this is: This is the season when the Father is speaking about the future to the "great house"[16] (all the ethnics of people that includes, but is not limited to leaders, good, bad, rich, poor, bond, and free).

And just like Pharaoh, they are people who inquire of the forbidden spirits who energizes false prophets, magicians, and wise men of Egypt to have them interpret their dreams. There is only one catch. Magicians, palm-readers, false prophets, et cetera cannot interpret a dream that really comes from God. Dreams or visions from God can only be interpreted by God's apostolic and prophetic ministries.

---

[16] Pharaoh is defined as "great house" by Strong's Concordance. Thus, Pharaoh can symbolize a great mass (house) of people (2 Timothy 2:20).

*Genesis 41:8, NIV: In the morning, his mind (lit., spirit) was troubled, so he sent for all the **magicians and wise men** of Egypt. Pharaoh told them his dreams, **but no one could interpret them for him.***

Pharaoh's mind (lit; spirit) was troubled due to the dream God gave him. In like manner, God has given, is giving and will give the people in the world dreams and their spirits are and will be "troubled" within them. However, some still refuse to acknowledge God, or they only seek for interpretation from who they are familiar with. Therefore, they go to false prophets, palm readers, witches, diviners, psychics, and so on to get the interpretation just like Pharaoh. But "no one could interpret" the dreams they had. God's dreams are, on the most part, "un-interpretable" to those who are false!

The Living God is the only person who can interpret a dream given by Him. It follows that if false prophets, palm readers, psychics, necromancers, witches, and wizards can interpret a dream, that dream did not come from God. Only "The Prophet", Jesus, who is in us—can interpret a dream given by God. Therefore, if a palm reader, psychic, or diviners ever interpreted something for you and said, "God gave you that dream," it is a lie. God did not give you that dream, because when God gives a dream, only an apostle or prophet through the Spirit of Lord can interpret it.[17] Amen!

*Genesis 41:15, NIV: Pharaoh said to Joseph, "I had a dream, and no one can interpret it. But I have heard it said of you that when you hear a dream **you can interpret it."***

*Genesis 41:16, NIV: **"I cannot do it,"** Joseph replied to Pharaoh, "but God will give Pharaoh the answer he desires."*

---

[17] Compare Daniel 2

Joseph acknowledged that he could not interpret the dream, either "but God will give Pharaoh the answer he desires." The Spirit of the living God gives the interpretation through his apostles and prophets in this age (Ephesians 3:5). One of the meanings of "apostle" is "sent one." Joseph who is a type of Jesus and a type of an apostle who was "sent" to Egypt. "And he **sent** a man before them — Joseph, sold as a slave" (Psalm 105:17).

The word "sent" is translated as "apostello" in the Septuagint (LXX) — the Greek translation of the Hebrew Bible that Jesus and the early apostles used. "Apostello", according to Vines Expository Dictionary, is akin to "apostolos" (an apostle); and according to Strong's Concordance "apostolos" is derived from "apostello." Therefore, Joseph foreshadowed the apostolic ministry of Jesus and apostles in general. God "sent" Joseph into Egypt, via slavery, to be an apostolic interpreter of the dreams of God (compare Philippians 2:7, NIV relative to Jesus becoming a "servant," which is also translated as a "slave"). Joseph, an apostle, interpretation insured better planning for the famine to come. Joseph's interpretation did not prevent the famine; it allowed the country to prepare for the worse.

God's mysteries are still being revealed **to/in** His holy apostles and prophets or interpreted **by** his holy apostles and prophets according to Ephesians 3:5-6 and Amos 3:7. Thus, there is also apostolic and prophetic directive for this generation relative to the famine to come, to also include, but not limited a "famine of haring the words of the Lord" (Amos 8:11). It was God in His sovereignty who "called for a famine upon the land" in the days of Joseph (Psalm 105:16).

In the case of Joseph, He was in place to give an interpretation which preserved the peoples. Crises are occurring and will occur in the world. Therefore, adjust your future accordingly, just as the Egyptians prepared for the famine through a prophet's interpretation.

In the Old Testament only Joseph, a sent one (an apostle), and Daniel, a prophet, could interpret the mysteries of God. Joseph and Daniel interpreted the mysterious dreams of kings (Genesis 41: 25-32, Daniel 2). So likewise, in this age, apostles and prophets will understand the mysteries of God. They will be able to interpret that which is dreamed and that which is written.

Ephesians 3:4-6, NIV: *⁴In reading this, then, you will be able to understand my insight into the mystery of Christ, ⁵ which was not made known to men in other generations **as it has now been revealed** by (Gk.; in) the Spirit **to God's holy apostles and prophets**. ⁶This mystery is that through the gospel the Gentiles are heirs together with Israel, members together of one body, and sharers together in the promise in Christ Jesus.*

Revelation 1:1, NIV: The revelation of Jesus Christ, which God gave him to show his servants what must soon take place. He made it known by sending his angel to his servant John,

*Revelation 10:7, NIV: But in the days when the seventh angel is about to sound his trumpet, the mystery of God will be accomplished, just **as he announced** to his servants the **prophets.***

*Amos 3:7, NIV: Surely the Sovereign LORD does nothing without revealing his plan to his servants **the prophets.***

Daniel had the ability to interpret dreams and prophetic things prewritten (Daniel 1-2; Daniel 9). Joseph, an apostle of God, was also able to define dreams that astrologers could not solve. Likewise, God has apostles and prophets today who can "discern the … times" (Matthew 16:1-4; Genesis 41; Daniel 2; Esther 1:13; 1 Chronicles 12:32).

Remember, when something is from the Lord Jesus, none of the false prophets or false apostles will be able to interpret it. They are limited like Jannes and Jambres. Jannes and Jambres could only duplicate three out of the ten miracles Moses demonstrated. So likewise, false prophets can only interpret dreams from Satan. They are limited. They cannot understand or interpret the dream and writing of the Spirit of Jesus (1 Corinthians 2:6-10). One of the reasons is that the answers to God's visions and writing are too deep in God. Only God's sons and daughters are allowed in the deep things of God through the Holy Spirit (1 Corinthians 2:9-10).

INTERPRETATION IS IN GOD'S WOMB

Daniel 2:17-18, NIV:1⁷ Then Daniel returned to his house and explained the matter to his friends Hananiah, Mishael and Azariah. ¹⁸ He urged them to plead for mercy from the God of heaven concerning **this mystery**, *so that he and his friends might not be executed with the rest of the wise men of Babylon.*

Nebuchadnezzar had a dream and was troubled (Daniel 2:1). Again, this may explain why some in this age are so troubled and seeking psychics and wizards. God is speaking to them [Romans 10:18; Colossians 1:6 and 1:23]; but they, like Nebuchadnezzar, are forgetting. Nebuchadnezzar sent for the magicians, enchanters, astrologers, and soothsayers to interpret the dream for him. The world is doing the same thing. However, as it was in Nebuchadnezzar's case, a prophet's interpretation was necessary.

Nebuchadnezzar required the potential interpreter to tell Nebuchadnezzar his own dream and the interpreter had to interpret the dream with no information from the king. In addition, before Daniel even interpreted Nebuchadnezzar's dream, the verdict for the false diviners who could not "make alive" the kings' dream was death (Daniel 2:2-11)! Of course, the false prophets could not, so the king ordered the false prophets be executed (Daniel 2: 12-14). However, "Daniel spoke with wisdom and tact" (Daniel 2:14c).

Daniel requested that an extension of time be granted to seek for the interpretation (Daniel 2:15-16). Daniel then went to his friends and urged them to "pray for **mercy** from the God of heaven." It is from this statement I will show you some truth concerning the womb of God. Daniel "urged them to plead for **mercy** from the God of heaven **concerning this mystery**" dream (Daniel 2:18).

"Mercy," in the text is defined as **"womb as cherishing"** according to Strong's Concordance. This lets us know that Daniel and his friends sought **the spiritual womb** of God — His heart and Spirit. The answer to every mystery is in the womb of God. False prophets are limited to what they can interpret, because they are not allowed into the womb of God. They are from the seed of Satan, and that which is satanic is destined for the lake of lightning and eternal fire (John 8:44; Matthews 25:41; Revelation 19:20). They cannot enter the spiritual womb of God unless they get saved. All true prophets must hear from the heart of God (Genesis 8: 21) and/or the womb of God to have the correct interpretation.

Daniel 2:19-20, NIV: [19]*During the night **the mystery** was **revealed** to Daniel **in a vision**. Then Daniel praised the God of heaven* [20] *and said: "Praise be to the name of God for ever and ever; wisdom and power are his.*

Daniel sought the spiritual womb of God, that which God will birth or plans to in the earth. The mystery was revealed to the prophet in a vision. This is filled with truth.

Principle: If something is unknown to you seek God's womb. He will reveal the mystery to you in the night seasons.

God revelation of mysteries will release worship in you to the heavenly Father. You will realize and say that "wisdom and power are His." With that said, remember that some of the many ways that God is using to reveal His secrets to the world are the voices of dreams, visions, and open vision (Genesis 41; Daniel 2; Daniel 4; Daniel 5, Acts 10). However, some are forgetting and/or do not understand the visions because some visions come as a language that only prophets and apostles can understand or interpret (Acts 10; Daniel 5).

In addition, people are seeking interpretation from the false ones; and they are <u>not</u> getting the right answers. Therefore, some of the dreamers are full of rage and murder like Nebuchadnezzar. The Church must interpret for the world by using the prophetic—Revelation 19:10c—as a "tool" to cause the "Nebuchadnezzars" of the world to worship living God of Jesus, the God of the Church. Listen to what the king said after Daniel revealed the truth. *"The king said to Daniel, "Surely your God is the God of gods and the Lord of kings and a revealer of mysteries, for you were able to reveal this mystery" (Daniel 2:47).*

The world, like Nebuchadnezzar, will acknowledge that Jesus is the God of gods, He is the Lord of kings as a result of prophetic interpreting that gives understanding (compare 1 Corinthians 14:25). The Prophet's interpretation will bring worship to God's sovereignty. Amen! People will worship the living God because "you were able to reveal this mystery" The key is to know that only God can give the interpretation as we seek His heart.

THE HEART OF GOD

*Genesis 8:21, NIV: **The LORD** smelled the pleasing aroma and **said in his heart:** "Never again will I curse the ground because of man, even though every inclination of his heart is evil from childhood. And never* *again will I destroy all living creatures, as I have done.*

One of the keys to hearing is to seek the Lord by through "all kinds of prayer and requests," in the Spirit (Ephesians 6:18). The Father, in His sovereign timing, will allow us to hear the heart of God. For example, we can understand that God made a covenant with Noah and humanity not to destroy the earth by water again because Noah, a man with like passion like us, was able to hear the heart of God. However, before Noah heard God's heart, he built an altar. The altar is symbolic of the sacrifice prayer.

*Genesis 8:20, NIV: Then Noah built an **altar** to the LORD and, taking some of all the clean animals and clean birds, he sacrificed burnt offerings on it.*

After the flood of judgment, Noah "built an altar to the LORD." He built prayer and it "smelled sweet" to God. The Bible says that prayer is as sweet incense (Psalm 141:2; Revelation 5:8; Revelation 8:1-5). This incense is the sweet smell of prayer that ascends into God's nose.

*Revelation 5:8, NIV: And when he had taken it, the four living creatures and the twenty-four elders fell down before the Lamb. Each one had a harp, and they were holding **golden bowls** full of **incense, which are the prayers of the saints**.*

Prayers are incense. The altar that Noah built was a type of prayer to God. He offered, literally, "ascending offerings" on this altar. That is, the Hebrew word for burnt offerings means "a step as ascending" (Strong's # 5930). The root word for means to "ascend." This shows us that we must ascend in prayer, through the sacrifice of Jesus Christ and His ascension, so we can hear the heart of God. Noah's offering of prayer ascended to God, and it was sweet like incense to God. The result was: God allowed Noah to hear His heart.

*Genesis 8:21, NIV: The LORD smelled the pleasing aroma and **said in his heart:** "Never again will I curse the ground because of man, even though every inclination of his heart is evil from childhood. And never again will I destroy all living creatures, as I have done."*

Did you hear what I heard? Noah heard the **heart** of God. **"The LORD ... said in His heart."** If he did not hear God's heart, the writer could not have recorded what we just read in the verse above. Noah heard God's heart. God spoke in His own heart and decreed a covenant for the people of the earth. This is significant.

There are things that may never be heard until we build a lifestyle dependent on prayer to the living God, through the sacrifice of Jesus Christ and His ascension! We must build an altar of persistent prayer in our homes. The secrets of God are revealed from His Holy Spirit (the spiritual heart and/or spiritual womb of God). We must "ascend" in prayer like the burnt offerings; and as we ascend in the Spirit, we will understand the mysteries of God (2 Corinthians 12). Men ruled by Babylon, like Belshazzar, cannot understand the writings of God, especially, the handwritings of judgment (Daniel 5). Men of prayer who seek the womb of God, they can understand. Daniel exemplified this fully. He had developed a prayer life of three times a day: *"Three times a day he got down on his knees and **prayed, giving thanks** to his God"* (Daniel 6:10).

Daniel apparently learned from the first experience that the womb or heart of God is the way to interpreting. This dedication for years, probably 70, plus years, led to the interpreting of the final judgment on Babylon. An application for God Church is that it is God's apostles and prophets who are declaring the fall of Babylon by interpreting the books of Revelation, Zechariah, Daniel, etc.

THE INSCRIPTION OF JUDGMENT

*Daniel 5:5-6, NIV: 5Suddenly **the fingers of a human hand** appeared and **wrote** on the plaster of the wall, near the lampstand in the royal palace. The king watched the hand as it wrote. 6 His face turned pale, and he was so frightened that his knees knocked together, and his legs gave way.*

Belshazzar was having a party drinking wine (symbolic of blood, Revelation 17:6) from the goblets (symbolic of God vessels) of the temple of God (Daniel 5:1-4 with 2 Corinthians 3:16). This was an offence to God. Therefore, God sent the writing of "sudden" judgment. *"**Suddenly** the fingers of a human hand appeared and wrote on the plaster of the wall, near the lampstand in the royal palace"* (Daniel 5: 5). This caused a panic in the king and his men. Belshazzar did the same thing Pharaoh, Nebuchadnezzar, and the children of this age do. *"The king called out for the enchanters, astrologers and diviners"* (Daniel 5:7). This action by the king was in vain.

The false prophets of Babylon are limited in their interpreting God's verdicts. Because they are fakes. Listen to the scripture: *"Then all the king's wise men came in, **but they could not** read the writing or tell the king what it meant"* (Daniel 5:8). The reason why they could not interpret the vision was because they were NOT of God. They do not have the "excellent Spirit" of God like Daniel and the saints of the living God (1 Corinthians 2:10; Daniel 5:12). Remember I said earlier, when a word, vision, dream, directions, and so on is from God, no false prophets, no astrological reading, no palm reading, no psychic reading, no wizards, nor diviners can interpret it. This is the same for the Holy Scriptures. False prophets and false apostles cannot properly understand God's writing, or "read the writing."

Therefore, if these kinds of people are reading for you, whatever they say is not from God. Why? They cannot "read the writing" from God. The only thing they can understand is that which is from demons (scribbles). The scripture calls it doctrines, teachings, of devils (1 Timothy 4:1). Things are going to get "frightening" for the world when their interpreters fail. They will have no choice but to turn to the Living God. His name is Jesus, King of kings and Lord of lords, the "only Potentate!" He is blessed forever more. With that said, the mother queen advised Belshazzar: *"Call for Daniel, and he will tell you what the writing means" (Daniel 5:12, last part).*

True apostles and prophets must be "called" and will be called to give understanding concerning the mystery of Babel's Judgment (Revelation 16:19-17:1 with Daniel 5:12). The angel gave the apostle John the revelation of the judgment of the great prostitute—Mystery Babylon (Revelation 17:1-5). The Spirit of God gave Daniel the interpretation of the writing concerning Babylon of his time. Those who walk in the Spirit will interpret the writing of God (Galatians 5:25, 1 Corinthians 2:14-16).

Principle: It will be the apostolic and prophetic team that will understand and interpret the mystery of judgment against Mystery Babylon.

EXAMPLES OF GOD'S WARNING OF IMMINENT JUDGMENT

1988, God warned me of a coming judgment to America. I was translated into the Spirit of God. In Him, God spoke to me in the secret place of thunder (Psalm 81:7).

I saw a huge eagle in flight, high in the clouds. The clouds were nimbus clouds. The color scheme of the eagle was as the flag of the United States of America. As I watched the eagle flying in a focused majestic flight, with its large wings pushing through the nimbus clouds in the heights, I heard the "sound" of thunders.

However, as I continued to listen, the sound of the thunders became a "voice" of thunders. I heard the thundering, yet a gentle thundering voice say, "Judgment, judgment, judgment…" As I heard this voice of thunders repeating with gentle peals.

On April 25, 2002, the lord woke me up early that morning. I got on my knees to pray; and I saw Jimmy Swaggart[18] and heard his name. I saw what he had accomplished as an evangelist. I then saw what he had become after the exposure of his participation in impure sexuality with prostitutes; and his repetition of the act that he was accused of after he apparently refused discipline by his peers. I also saw and heard how he has become a byword in the land among the saved and unsaved. I then began to pray for him that he would be restored. (I thought that was the reason the Lord brought him to my attention).

However, as I prayed, the Holy Spirit stopped me, and I felt my ears dilate and the Holy Spirit said, **"Others, who have done like he has done, will also be exposed."** I then heard Him say; He (the Holy Spirit) will be removing priests from the earth (Acts 5; Ezekiel 9). My presumptuous prayer for Swaggart ended. I continued to listen as I saw the Pope, and I sensed that God was about to remove him by death also; as I continued to look, I saw what appeared to be Eli. Then I heard the Scriptures in my ears **"I will do things in your day that will cause the ears of people to tingle"** – again, during this encounter my ears were literally being dilated to hear (I could feel and see the dilation).

It appears that Eli represented the Pope who like Eli did not correct his sons who were priests; therefore, God allowed Eli (a type of the Pope) to die, and God killed Eli's sons (priests)? Within two weeks of the vision from the Lord, I heard on the

---

[18] Note: I mention his name only because I heard his name, specifically in prayer. I have nothing against Jimmy Swaggart; and like most Christians in America, I used to listen to his teaching and singing in the mid-1980s.

news how a Catholic priest was shot for a situation related to inappropriate sexuality. Another priest hanged himself for similar reasons. Months later, another priest got killed in prison. Ironically, Pope John Paul II, died three years later in the same month (April) the Lord showed me this vision.

In 1992 I was in a season of multiple extensive fasting. On this fast, it was about the 9th day of the fast, and it was my first fast going this long. Being hungry, my flesh was without strength, and as I sat on the sofa waiting for Judith to fix some soup for me, I saw a vision and heard a voice say, **"The way is being made for the spirit of Greece."** I then heard a voice say, **"A great tragedy shall happen in America,"** as I heard the voice speak, **I saw a president standing upon a pile of rubble exactly as President Bush did after 9/11.** I then heard the voice say, **"After the tragedy, I will bring forth the Boy Scouts."**

REVELATION IN THE SPIRIT OF GOD

Revelation 1:10-11, NIV: [10] *On the Lord's Day* ***I was in the Spirit,*** *and I heard behind me a loud voice like a trumpet,* [11] *which said: "Write on a scroll what you see and send it to the seven churches: to Ephesus, Smyrna, Pergamum, Thyatira, Sardis, Philadelphia and Laodicea."*

John **"was** in the Spirit" on the Lord's Day (not Sunday as supposed by some). The word "was" is the Greek word "ginomai" and is defined as "a prolongation and middle voice form of a primary verb; to cause to be ("gen"-erate), i.e. (reflexively) to become (come into being), used with great latitude (literal, figurative, intensive, etc.):" [Strong's # 1096]. It is translated "born" in the New International Version.

Galatians 4:4, NIV: But when the time had fully come, God sent his Son, born of a woman, ***born*** *under law…*

The point is this: John was **birthed** into the Spirit realm. He "became" in the Spirit. He was "caused to be" in the Spirit. Therefore, the writings of Revelation are <u>spiritual</u>. It can only be interpreted by those in the Spirit God. I will say like Paul, *"⁴In reading this, then, you will be able to understand my insight into the mystery of Christ, ⁵which was not made known to men in other generations as it has now been **revealed by the Spirit (lit.; in the Spirit)** to God's holy apostles and prophets"* (Ephesians 3:4-5, NIV). Those "born" from above can "see the kingdom of God" (John 3:3). John was invited to go up to heaven, because Jesus wanted to "show" him some things that will take place (Revelation 4:1). The Scripture said, "At once I was in the Spirit."

*Revelation 4:1-2, NIV: ¹After this I looked, and there before me was **a door standing open in heaven.** And the voice I had first heard speaking to me like a trumpet said, "**Come up here,** and I will show you what must take place after this." ²**At once I was in the Spirit,** and there before me was a throne in heaven with someone sitting on it.*

Did you catch that? He was invited to heaven, and at once he was in the Spirit. Thus, heaven is in the Spirit. Heaven is not millions of miles away. Heaven is right next to you. Paul said we are to "walk in the Spirit" (Galatians 5:16 and 5:25). Walking in the Spirit also has to do with the mind (mindset). Revelation 4:1-2 lets us know that heaven is in the Spirit. Therefore, when we walk in the spirit we are walking in heaven. When we walk in the Spirit, or we are birthed in the Spirit; we can "see" heaven. Yes! Yes! Yes!

It was after John was birthed into the Spirit that he was able to see the Lamb of God open the book of Revelation to him. The book was sealed. God gave it to Jesus (Revelation 1:1) Jesus opened it and gave it to John at God's choosing. And God did all this through His Spirit (Revelation 4:2).

1 Corinthians 2:9-10, NIV: ⁹However, as it is written: "No eye has seen, no ear has heard, no mind has conceived what God has prepared for those who love him" – ¹⁰but **God has revealed it to us by his Spirit.** *The Spirit searches all things, even the deep things of God.*

Revelation 4:2, NIV: **At once I was in the Spirit,** *and there before me was a throne in heaven with someone sitting on it.*

Revelation 5:1-5, NIV: ¹Then I saw in the right hand of him who sat on the throne a scroll with writing on both sides and sealed with seven seals. ²And I saw a mighty angel proclaiming in a loud voice, "Who is worthy to break the seals and open the scroll?" ³But no one in heaven or on earth or under the earth could open the scroll or even look inside it. ⁴I wept and wept because no one was found who was worthy to open the scroll or look inside. ⁵Then one of the elders said to me, "Do not weep! See, the Lion of the tribe of Judah, the Root of David, has triumphed. He is able to open the scroll and its seven seals."

It was in the Spirit that John saw the scroll sealed with seven seals. No one was found worthy to open the scroll or look inside. There are some things that are seen by the populous, yet the understanding is sealed by God. Nebuchadnezzar, Belshazzar, and Pharaoh experienced this firsthand. However, those who are spiritual and elected by God's graceful Lamb will be allowed to see, know again, interpret, and understand that which was once unlawful to utter or uninterpretable (2 Corinthians 12:4).

The "elect", the Church, of the Lamb of God will be able to understand mysteries that were once hidden (Revelation 5:5, Colossians 1:25-26, Ephesians 3: 1-5). This will be done through The Holy Spirit's to His holy apostles and prophets. With the understanding that everything apostles and prophets receive is for the benefit and maturing of the Body of Christ. Listen to the language of Paul again: *"²Surely you have heard about the administration of* **God's grace that was given to me for you,** *³that is,* **the mystery made known to me by revelation,** *as I have already written briefly"* *(Ephesians 3:2-3, NIV).*

Jesus will also give interpretation, through His Church, the dreams/writings that the world (Egypt, Babylon, the ignorant, etc.) could not previously understand (Daniel 5, Genesis 41, Acts 8:25-39). One of the purposes is to make known His death, burial, and resurrection to those who need salvation, in addition to future events that God has planned to occur. It will take Jesus being revealed in the right way to interpret the dreams and visions that cannot be interpreted by the false prophets of the world.

Finally, my brothers, walk in the Spirit of Jesus, seek the womb of God, and do not fulfill the lust of this sinful generation. Seek the Lord Jesus and abstain from the false ones. They may "war" against the truth but remember, *"...The Lamb will overcome them because he is Lord of lords and King of kings – and with him will be his called, chosen and faithful followers" (Revelation 17:14).*

Be faithful to the Lord Jesus Christ. The grace of the Lord Jesus fills your heart. Amen!

Other Books

Wisdom from Above, by Judith Peart
Procreation, Understanding Sex, and Identity, by Judith Peart
100 Nevers, by Judith Peart
The Shattered and the Healing by Judith Peart
The Lamb, by Donald Peart
Jesus' Resurrection, Our Inheritance, by Donald Peart.
Sexuality, By Donald Peart
Forgiven 490 Times, by Donald Peart w/Judith Peart!
The Days of the Seventh Angel, By Donald Peart
The Torah (The Principle) of Giving, by Donald Peart
The Time Came, by Donald Peart
The Last Hour, the First Hour, the Forty-Second Generation, by Donald Peart
Vision Real, by Donald Peart
The False Prophet, Alias, Another Beast V1, by Donald Peart
"the beast," by Donald Peart
Son of Man Prophesy Against the false prophet, by Donald Peart
The Red Dragon's Tail—The Prophets who Teach Lies, by Donald Peart
The Work of Lawlessness Revealed, by Donald Peart
When the Lord Made the Tempter, by Donald Peart
Examining Doctrine, Volume 1, by Donald Peart
Exousia, Your God Given Authority, by Donald Peart
The Numbers of God, by Donald Peart
The Completions of the Ages … by Donald Peart
The Revelation of Jesus Christ, by Donald Peart
Jude—Translation and Commentary, by Donald Peart
Obtaining the Better Resurrection, by Donald Peart
Manifestations from Our Lord Jesus …by Donald and Judith Peart).
Obtaining the Better Resurrection, by Donald Peart
The New Testament, Dr. Donald Peart Exegesis
The Spirit and Power of John, the Baptist by Dr. Donald Peart
The Shattered and the Healing by Judith Peart
Is She Married to a Husband? by Donald Peart
The Ugliest Man God Made by Donald Peart
Does Answering the Call of God Impact Your Children? by Donald Peart
Victory Out-of-the Beast-the Harvest of the Earth by Donald Peart
The Order of Melchizedek by Donald Peart
Ezekiel, the House, the City, the Land (Interpreting the Patterns) by Donald Peart

Contact Information:

Crown of Glory Ministries
P.O. Box 1041 Randallstown, MD 21133
donaldpeart7@gmail.com